Gilding the Ghetto
The state and the poverty experiments

CDP

Introduction

It costs so little to enjoy this DOLPHIN Luxury Shower

* You can have six Dolphin Showers

Spend £100m a year on inner cities—Tories

By JOHN LEWIS
Birmingham Post Political Correspondent

The spending of £100 million a year over the next five, or even ten, years — quadrupling the present aid on special projects for the inner areas of cities — is urged by the Tory Reform Group.

The findings of a working party of the Conservative pressure group, led by Mr. David Lane, chairman-designate of the Commission for Racial Equality, follow closely on the admission by Mr. Peter Shore, the Environment Secretary, that more resources must be devoted to inner cities. The official Conservative Party strategy, to be unveiled in the next week or so, is likely to reach a similar conclusion.

A STRATEGY FOR CITY LIFE

Peter Wilsher and *Rosemary Righter* describe why action for our cities is an urgent national priority

Britain's cities are rotting at the core. Even in such traditionally pleasant spots as Exeter and Edinburgh, the tell-tale signs are beginning to show. Boarded-up businesses and derelict sites; slum pockets and vandalised high-rise blocks; shrinking job opportunities, lengthening unemployment queues, rising welfare bills.

For years these symptoms of decay appeared to be largely confined to the poorer and nastier parts of the great northern conurbations – Tyneside, Clydeside and Merseyside – and to most official minds the appropriate solution was summed up in the phrase 'slum clearance'. Only now, when 2200 acres of 'prime city land' is lying vacant in central Liverpool, when inner London has lost 386,000 jobs in the last decade, and even Brighton and Hove have more than 6000 people living in 'multiply deprived' areas, does the Government appreciate that it has a national crisis on its hands.

The change has been swift and dramatic. It was first realised 10 years ago that some inner-city districts were becoming chronic generators of deprivation and poverty. Whitehall's only answer then was a £15 million a year Urban Aid Programme, described by one sociologist as "urban first aid – tentative, minuscule, fragmented and largely abortive". But now the Prime Minister has set up a

with the optimistic planning act of the late 1940s, which gave councils totally new powers to remake their war-blasted cities. For the next 30 years they used these for enthusiastic slum-demolition campaigns and the erection of vast estates and tower blocks – the notorious 'raze and rise' era.

Three things went basically wrong during this period. One was that demolition typically outpaced new construction; council waiting-lists lengthened and over-crowding persisted. Even now, there are more than 53,000 London households living in 'severely overcrowded' conditions (1½ people or more to a room). Clydeside, a quarter the size, has nearly 59,000. Another was the primacy given to architects' ideas on how people should live. They isolated them from the noise of the streets, insulated them from traffic on lonely 'pedestrian walkways' and ignored the hell 16th-floor living can be for anybody with young children. And the third was the failure to appreciate the social cost of breaking up communities and separating people geographically from their jobs. Significantly, the 1971 census analysis shows that the areas with the worst overcrowding and unemployment are also those with the highest density of (mostly new) local authority housing.

Towards the end of 1976 among the endless reminders of Britain's economic predicament another theme was brought to public attention: the urban crisis. 'Task force needed for the cities', Shelter and others insisted, and the Secretary of State for the Environment gave the news official weight: 'If cities fail, so to a large extent does our society. That is the urgency of tackling the problem; and why it has to be of concern to everyone in this land.' (Peter Shore, 17.9.76). The *Sunday Times* picked up the theme, 'Britain's cities are rotting at the core', it announced, 'but now the Prime Minister has set up a top level ministerial committee led by Peter Shore to establish a whole new policy for our cities'. (28.11.76) The urban crisis was presented as acute, demanding immediate attention, moreover it was apparently a new problem to which new solutions must be found.

For the government though it was no new issue. Ten years ago many of its leading members were part of an earlier administration which set about a very similar task with a series of experimental programmes to combat what was then called 'urban deprivation'. Compared with the scale of the USA's Poverty Program of the same period the money may have been rather small, nevertheless £80m was poured into the experiment. The Urban Programme, Educational Priority Areas, CDPs, Inner Area Studies, Quality of Life projects and many more like them were seeded all over the country, employing scores of people as the new professionals of deprivation, its study and, in theory, its cure. Some of the projects are still running.

Yet today there is an official silence about these programmes of the late 1960s and early seventies. A striking silence. There is no mention of what they revealed, whether they succeeded in their task or how far the government of J. Callaghan Prime Minister has been able to learn from the initiatives of J. Callaghan Home Secretary. What, in fact, happened is unclear. For academics, researchers and civil servants looking for clues there are many heavy volumes and long reports from the various separate projects, lying around in government offices and weighing down library shelves. For the 'general public' and particularly for those people on whom the 'experiments' were conducted no account is given. Today's 'new' rhetoric of inner city crisis appears to begin on a clean sheet.

This report goes back to the early stage. Written by a group of workers from the National Community Development Project it tries to make sense of the spate of government 'poverty initiatives' beginning in 1968 of which CDP was a part. It is written from inside but, we hope, for an outside world. It comes from our own experience as some of the state's 'poverty' workers, and from the doubts that experience raised in our minds about what our employers were really intending.

Why this kind of programme? What is it for?

Govt action to halt decay of city centres

by STANLEY SPARKS

THE GOVERNMENT is to act to stop the life blood draining out of Britain's major cities. Environment Secretary Mr. Peter Shore today announced a nurgent review of Government policies of dispersal of homes and jobs from city centres in a bid to halt their decay.

He also hinted that the cities would be getting a bigger slice of available Government cash to stop the rot.

He said that all major cities have lost populations over the past 15 years and went on: "What is more worrying is the unbalanced nature of the migration with a high number of skilled workers and young people moving

This leaves the inner areas with a disproportionate share of unskilled and semi-skilled workers, of unemployment, of one-parent families, of concentrations of immigrant communities and over-crowded and inadequate housing.

Mr. Shore, who has been given special responsibility by the Prime Minister for

Ten years on: the urban crisis rediscovered, 1976. Led by Mr Peter Shore *(top)* **Secretary of State for the Environment and his opposition colleagues, orchestrated by the press**

The CDP story

The Home Office, with James Callaghan as Home Secretary, embarked on CDP in 1969. The idea was to collaborate with local authorities in setting up local projects, each with a five-year lifespan as 'a neighbourhood-based experiment aimed at finding new ways of meeting the needs of people living in areas of high social deprivation'. There were to be twelve projects, and these were eventually located in *Batley*, West Yorkshire, *Benwell*, West Newcastle, *Canning Town*, East London, *Cleator Moor*, Cumbria, *Glyncorrwg*, West Glamorgan, *Hillfields*, Coventry, *Vauxhall*, Liverpool, *North Shields*, Tyneside, *Clarksfield*, Oldham, *Paisley*, Glasgow, *Saltley*, Birmingham, *Southwark*, South-East London.

Their brief rested on three important assumptions. Firstly, that it was the 'deprived' themselves who were the cause of 'urban deprivation'. Secondly, the problem could best be solved by overcoming these people's apathy and promoting self-help. Thirdly, locally-based research into the problems would serve to bring about changes in local and central government policy.

A few months' field-work in areas suffering long-term economic decline and high unemployment was enough to provoke the first teams of CDP workers to question the Home Office's original assumptions. There might certainly be in these areas a higher proportion of the sick and the elderly for whom a better co-ordination of services would undoubtedly be helpful, but the vast majority were ordinary working-class men and women who, through forces outside their control, happened to be living in areas where bad housing conditions, redundancies, lay-offs, and low wages were commonplace.

Despite this, the early teams remained faithful to their brief at first. They set up multi-disciplinary teams and specialist projects, and submitting detailed reports on industrial change, opportunities for school leavers and failures of housing-policy they waited for a response. Nothing happened. Central government departments were either hostile or, more often, uninterested. Soon the other part of the brief, the plan to mobilise community self-help, began to bring out the real contradictions at the heart of the CDP notion. As the teams began in earnest to work and organise with local tenants and action groups over questions of housing or welfare rights they found themselves drawn into direct conflict with councillors and officials of the local authorities — the very people who, in part at least, were their employers.

The authorities found themselves under fire. Tenants groups were able to draw on research and information back-up from the CDPs to criticise council policies and present their own proposals, while in Liverpool CDP, for example, adult education workers became drawn into a political campaign against the Housing Finance Bill in 1972. Local politicians were not slow to respond. In 1974 there was conflict between project and local authority at Batley over the funding of a locally-run action centre which led first to the resignation of some of the CDP workers and

finally to the total closure of the project. In Cleator Moor activity around welfare rights and community issues roused the antagonism of local Tory politicians who eventually managed to bring the project to a premature end in early 1976, while in November 1976 Birmingham's new Tory council, enraged by an article on racism and unemployment in the Saltley project's Urdu newspaper, came near to closing it down. Other projects have also been threatened with closure either because of specific issues or general hostility from councillors and officers to the CDP ways of working. To many of them the CDP workers were little short of 'political agitators'.

Below: **1968, J. Callaghan, Home Secretary, and first signs of CDP.** *Opposite,* **CDP underway: the Birmingham project's base in Saltley.**

COVENTRY TO HAVE 'GUINEA PIG' AREA EXPERIMENT

Evening Telegra[ph]

A DISTRICT of Coventry—p[art] of four areas in Britain chos[en for] a new Government expe[rimental] development.

This was announced in [Coven]try last night by Mr. R[ichard] Crossman, Secretary of St[ate for] Social Services, speaking [at] Lanchester College of Tec[hnology].

Mr. Crossman said th[e] "action" experiment [which] marked a new departure [in the] development of the social [services] would be called the [Community] Development Pro[ject].

"It involves and welding [together] different ser[vices] central or [...]

'All-in' social services trial

Welfare Correspondent

[The] Government is to [l]ater this month its [experime]ntal community [developm]ent project in areas [of] social need.

[The proj]ect will unite all the [so]cial services in a [...] effort to find [those who] are not now getting [the]y need, and makes a [...] major recommenda[tion of the] Seebohm committee, [but no] final decision has [been ann]ounced.

[To st]art in four areas, [Sou]thwark in London, [it will ev]entually be extended [to bi]g cities in the Mid[lands and] the North. Central [grants will] come from London, [the p]rogramme will be [ov]er about five years.

[...]an, Secretary for Social [ser]vices, will coordinate the work [but] the actual direction will be [in] the hands of Mr Callaghan, [Ho]me Secretary.

Mr Crossman has called the [pr]oject "a new departure in the [de]velopment of the social [se]rvices." With all the local and

Blac[...]

After the meet[ing] [...]an said that [...] [p]robably be the ar[...] [b]ut he would not [...] [t]hree.

Earlier Mr Cross[man]

Local conflict was not the only kind facing the projects. In the early phases the Home Office was content merely to distance itself from the experiment by relaxing central control and 'encouraging more local initiative'. But as the projects began to make links with the labour movement to organise nationally, and proclaim that the problems of urban poverty with which they were confronted, were the consequence of fundamental inequalities in the economic and political system, the Home Office's olympian detachment changed to a growing concern that CDP was out of control.

In 1973 a central CDP Information and Intelligence Unit had been set up, with a handful of central workers answerable to the teams, and the *Inter-Project Report* (1974) presented the changing perspectives of CDP. Inter-

project groups had also begun to meet and examine the common processes affecting the different areas. The result was a series of national CDP reports criticising local and central government policy, among them *the Poverty of the Improvement Programme, Whatever Happened to Council Housing? Profits against Houses* and *the Costs of Industrial Change.* In June 1974 the Home Office announced a Management Review of CDP: a new stage in the relationship had begun and the Home Office started actively seeking ways to close down or curtail project activities. Its first attempts were not a success. The projects mounted organised opposition to the Management Review's proposals for greater central control and the Home Office backed down. But by 1975 it was hinting to the local authorities that they should consider carefully

whether they could really continue to support CDP given the difficult financial circumstances.

Early 1976 brought a final direct attack. Six weeks after the central intelligence unit published the highly critical report on the government's public spending cuts, *Cutting the Welfare State (Who Profits)*, the Home Secretary ordered the closure of the unit. This in effect made it much more difficult for local projects to work together or produce shared conclusions and national documents. Today as the surviving projects go into their last phase the Home Office concentrates its efforts on salvaging what it can from the 'experiment' by tightening the timetable for final reports from the local projects. The projects themselves, now a long way from the position they began with, struggle to make sense of the insights they've gained and present these to a wider audience.

This report is part of that attempt. Though it is not an account *of* our experience — that is to be found in the various local and inter-project reports — it tries to locate and explain that experience in the context of the series of government moves of which CDP was one. These in turn can only be explained against the background of economic and social changes in the post-1945 years and particularly those of the 1960s. Perhaps we have raised more questions than we have been able to answer. Still we hope that our analysis will help to clarify for others as it has for us, the role of government in relation to both the demands of the economy and pressures from the working class, and the part that such programmes we describe here as the 'Poverty Programme' play in maintaining the status quo.

All a mistake? CDP under attack, 1976. Birmingham Council subsequently withdrew their threat *(below)* to close the Saltley project prematurely, but Cleator Moor *(opposite)* and the Information Unit *(bottom)* came to an end

Axe falls on urban projects

Bang goes another community plan

ANOTHER community development project is to close, following the recent Home Office circular telling local authorities that it was up to them whether or not their projects continued.

The Policy and Resources Committee of Cumbria County Council, which is Tory controlled, decided last week to end the Cleator Moor project.

The reason given is economy. But as the local authority grant was only £6,500 and the project attracted a Government grant of £100,000 this seems strange economics.

Project director Alan Tweedie said: "This is obviously a political decision. Many of our findings in the area affected a handful of members of the local power elite and presumably they felt threatened. Since they carry considerable political weight locally, we obviously never stood a chance."

Offers of support are pouring in, not the least from Copeland Borough Council, in which the CDP is situated, who were not informed that any such decision was being taken, let alone consulted, nor were local parish councils and organisations working alongside the CDP told anything either. No member of the CDP staff was allowed in to the meeting to defend its record.

Other CDP supporters are Dr. John Cunningham, the Labour MP for Whitehaven, Len Green, secretary of Cleator Moor Labour Party, and John Collingham, chairman of the CDP management Committee.

Cleator Moor CDP say: "We are drawing attention to the need for better housing, more and better jobs, decent treatment of the individual. Helping those who need help most — the elderly, sick, young, unemployed and low paid are being told their rights.

A petition is now being circulated calling on local people to support their CDP and supporters are asked to write to John Cunningham at the House of Commons and to T. J. R. Whitefield of Cumbria County Council, to lobby their local councillors, to write to the Press and to call in and offer what help they can.

Tory axe to end Saltley area project

Poverty reports 'gagged'

By PETER HILDREW

The Home Secretary, Mr Jenkins, has decided to close the information and intelligence unit which has been coordinating the work of the country's 13 community development projects, Staff at the unit, which is linked to the Centre for Environmental Studies in London, were advised by letter yesterday that their grant would be withdrawn from the end of April.

The head of the urban deprivation unit at the Home Office, Mr Gordon Wasserman, said the decision was due to "the present economic situation." But in a statement the staff immediately attacked the closure as a political move designed to 'protect the Government from embarrassing criticism.

In recent months, the unit has been responsible for publishing a series of critical reports based on the experience of the projects in various deprived parts of the country. Its latest document—published jointly with Counter-Information Services under the title "Cutting the Welfare State Profits?"—argues that public expenditure cuts will hit the poor worse and should be resisted. Other reports in preparation include one on unemployment and one on the social effects of council housing. The unit's director, Mr Mike Cantor, said last night he hoped it might still be possible to publish these before the funds run out.

The decision could not have come at a worse time for the projects, which are due to complete their work in the next 18 months and to submit reports on their experiences. The information unit for the community development projects was set up in 1973 cisely to draw together these reports and to give publicity to their findings. Workers on the projects felt that the lessons to be learned from their efforts might disappear without trace in Whitehall, where Home Office enthusiasm for the experiment rapidly waned.

The 12 projects were set up by the previous Labour Government in 1969, with the Home Office providing 75 per cent of the finance and the sponsoring local authority 25 per cent. Research teams were attached to each project, and those in Coventry and Liverpool have completed their work. Two more projects, at Batley in Yorkshire and Cleator Moor, Cumbria, are being wound up by the local councils, but the other eight, from Paisley to Tower Hamlets, are still in operation.

The budget for the information and intelligence unit and its five staff is £33,000 this year; in their statement the staff said that serious would

Grant cut closes deprivation unit

By Penny Symon

The Information and Intelligence Unit, which has become the focal point of the Government's Community Development Project, is closing because of an unexpected Home Office decision to discontinue its grant from April.

The unit, in Tavistock Place, Bloomsbury, has just received a copy of a letter from Mr Gordon Wasserman, head of the Urban Deprivation Unit at the Home Office, to the Centre for Environmental Studies, which administers the unit's grant. It says Mr Jenkins, Home Secretary, has reluctantly decided to discontinue the grant from April 30, because of the present economic situation, a reason which was rejected yesterday by Mr Michael Cantor, the unit's director.

"It is clear that the reason for the closure is not economic", he said. "The unit's budget for the current year is only £33,000."

The Community Development Project was set up by the Labour Government in 1969 as part of its urban programme. Its aim was to find new ways of meeting the needs of people living in areas of high social deprivation.

"Since May, 1975, the unit has sold about £3,500 worth of publications. The most recent on the cuts in the welfare state has sold out of its first printing of 8,000 copies, in less than two months", Mr Cantor said.

"That document criticised the Government's economic strategy and we feel the withdrawal of our grant is an attempt to stifle our criticisms."

6

Part one

The poverty programme

1 A Decade of projects

A handful of home secretaries: *top left,* **James Callaghan;** *right,* **Robert Carr;** *bottom left,* **Roy Jenkins;** *right,* **Merlyn Rees.** The Home Office led the field in urban deprivation but it was a series of official reports that triggered off the activity: *below,* **Lady Plowden and the Plowden Report,** *bottom* **the Seebohm Report.**

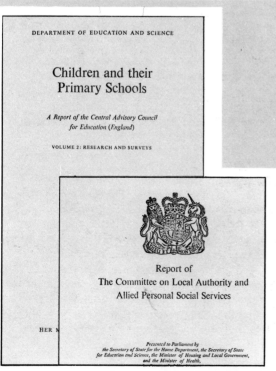

DEPARTMENT OF EDUCATION AND SCIENCE

Children and their
Primary Schools

*A Report of the Central Advisory Council
for Education (England)*

VOLUME 2: RESEARCH AND SURVEYS

Report of
The Committee on Local Authority and
Allied Personal Social Services

HER

*Presented to Parliament by
the Secretary of State for the Home Department, the Secretary of State
for Education and Science, the Minister of Housing and Local Government,
and the Minister of Health,*

When, in the sixties, the last wave of concern swept academics, politicians and the media into action over Britain's deteriorating older areas, the name of the problem as it was then identified was 'urban deprivation'.

It was a string of official reports with resonant names — Milner-Holland, Ingleby, Plowden, Seebohm — that first drew official attention to the new issue and insisted that more public money would have to be devoted to its solution. The 'problem' threatened to get worse, and with the whole structure of the Welfare State under increasing pressure the government was stung into action, launching a series of schemes and projects to test out possible new solutions on the ground.

Different government departments sponsored different projects. There was little central co-ordination. But the ideas were common and the organisation of the different schemes took very similar forms. It was an experiment— the word comes up again and again — conducted with very limited resources in a lot of separate laboratories. The central state drew in the local authorities, disregarding their traditional departmental boundaries. 'Citizen involvement' and 'participation' were other recurring themes. Most important, all the schemes took as their testing grounds, small, working-class districts of Britain's big cities and older industrial towns. These were the 'areas of special need' which had first come to the centre of official concern; soon they were being called 'pockets of deprivation'.

Sounding the alarm

The first sounds of the new alarm came from a series of commissions of enquiry set up by the government in the early 1960s. Though they had been designed to look into quite distinct subject areas — London's housing (Milner-Holland), children and young persons (Ingleby), primary education (Plowden), personal social services (Seebohm) — one after the other their reports came up with the same theme.

areas in which bad housing is concentrated should be designated as areas of special control in which bad living conditions would be attacked comprehensively, assisted by an enlargement of powers.
The Milner Holland Report: *Housing in Greater London,* 1965

positive discrimination . . . should favour schools in neighbourhoods where children are most severely handicapped by home conditions. The programme should be phased to make schools in the most deprived areas as good as the best in the country . . .

Some of these neighbourhoods have for generations been starved of new schools, new houses and new investment of every kind. Everyone knows this; but for year after year priority has been given to the New towns and New suburbs . . .

The Plowden Report: *Children and their Primary Schools*, 1966

We are convinced that designated areas of special need should receive extra resources, comprehensively planned . . .

The Seebohm Report: *Local Authority and allied personal services*, 1968

The small-scale, isolated area of 'special' deprivation, overwhelmingly in the older cities, became a fact of life — as report after report announced its existence. Something had to be done.

From reports to projects: the first wave

The first move to put these ideas into action came when changes were made in the Rate Support Grant. The intention was to give the authorities with the fewest resources and the greatest need more government aid than the others. This marked a considerable change in the principles on which central government resources had been allocated and paved the way for further 'positive discrimination' schemes.

During the same period with the new reports on housing, education and social services all presenting the problems and their potential solutions in terms of 'areas of special need', the idea was soon taken up by the local authorities too. These services did after all make up the bulk of their work and consume a substantial part of their budgets. By 1968 many councils had taken on new staff, special 'community workers', to co-ordinate aspects of their work in the target areas.

Meanwhile the development of these ideas had been paralleled by growing government concern at the problem of 'immigrants', meaning black immigrants in particular. When immigration from the Commonwealth had begun in the late 1940s successive governments had encouraged this painless solution to their labour shortage and been content to leave the task of settling in the new arrivals to the churches and voluntary organisations. In 1958 race riots in London's Notting Hill disturbed their calm and drew attention to Britain's growing black community. Blacks become linked with other 'deprived' people as a source of official concern.

A report by the Family Welfare Association recommending the appointment of community relations officers in boroughs with 'non-European' populations, brought the government into action during 1962 with the appointment of the Commonwealth Immigrants Advisory Council. It in turn recommended that the National Commit-

tee for Commonwealth Immigrants (NCCI) should be set up. As the government started cutting back the number of immigrants allowed into the country in 1965, it encouraged the NCCI to set up local committees and 'non-political' voluntary organisations with small amounts of money to finance local projects and foster 'integration' through language classes, play groups and other community activities. The pattern was repeated in 1968. At the same time as the Commonwealth Immigration Act was passed, further restricting immigration, the NCCI was re-organised as the Community Relations Commission and became responsible for overseeing the employment and training of Community Relations Officers to work with local committees.

URBAN AID

By 1968 ideas about how to tackle the problem had developed and the Urban Aid Programme appeared on the scene. 'The purpose of the programme', said James Callaghan, then Home Secretary, 'is to supplement the government's other social and legislative measures in order to ensure as far as we can that all our citizens have an equal opportunity in life'. (Hansard, 22.7.68) Introducing the legislation authorising the Urban Programme of which the major component was to be Urban Aid, he went on to elaborate. Its purpose was, he said

to provide for the care of our citizens who live in the poorest or most overcrowded parts of our cities and towns. It is intended to arrest, in so far as it is possible by financial means, and reverse the downward spiral which afflicts so many of these areas. There is a deadly quagmire of need and apathy.
Hansard, 2.12.68

The first Urban Programme Circular, sent out in October 1968, spelt it out:

The government proposed to initiate an urban programme of expenditure mainly on education, housing, health and welfare in areas of special social need. Those were localised districts which bear the marks of multiple deprivation, which may show itself, for example, by way of notable deficiencies in the physical environment, particularly housing; overcrowding of houses; family sizes above the average; persistent unemployment; a high proportion of children in trouble or in need of care; or a combination of these. A substantial degree of immigrant settlement would also be an important factor, though not the only factor, in determining the existence of special social need.
Urban Programme Circular No.1, October 1968

Responsibility for Urban Aid was located in the Community Relations Department of the Home Office, the department also responsible for the Community Relations Commission. The money made available for Urban Aid was not an extra government grant, but money already existing in the Rate Support Grant which was taken out of the general allocation and put into the Special Grant category. This allowed the government to have for the first time some direct control over what was going on 'at the grass roots'. Local authorities could apply for grants from this Special Grant for specific projects which could be financed for up to five years on a 75/25% basis.

As the local authorities grasped the new idea and sent back descriptions of the areas they regarded as being 'of special social need' the kinds of projects supported through the Urban Aid Programme widened in scope. From the nursery schools, day nurseries and children's homes, family advice centres and language classes for immigrants of the earlier phases, it had extended its embrace to many more informal kinds of organisation by the later phases. The Home Office actively encouraged local authorities to support autonomous forms of organisation that were already active in their areas. Women's Aid centres, holiday play schemes, housing and neighbourhood advice centres, family planning projects were all included in later phases of the Urban Aid Programme.

But though the range of projects has increased, the money available for new projects has not. In fact it has decreased in real terms, having stayed at around £4m a year. Many of the projects have been linked with other government policies, like nursery classes in conjunction with the Educational Priority Areas and housing advice centres in conjunction with General Improvement Areas. More recently Urban Aid money has been used to fund intermediate treatment projects for young offenders initiated by the Department of Health and Social Security.

In April 1974 the planned spending on overseas aid for Uganda (£2.3m) was diverted into immigrant projects and in July 1971 the Urban Aid Programme received £6m out of a special once only £160m government building programme to assist the building industry in economically depressed areas.

Urban Aid may have been by far the most extensive and expensive of the government's poverty initiatives but so far it has approved no more than £43.5m worth of a potential fund of £60m-£65m. Meanwhile there have been around five times more applications made than those granted. In 1971 for instance the London Borough of Lambeth submitted applications for projects to cost £103,500 — only £13,650 of this was approved.

EPA

There is not the kind of partnership between parents and teachers in relation to children that there should be in an ideal community. *Educational Priority* Vol.1, 1972

At about the same time as the Urban Aid Programme was being set up, the Department of Education and Science and the Social Science Research Council announced their Educational Priority Area (EPA) action-research project.

This formed part of the national programme of EPAs, the offspring of the Plowden Report, which local authorities were responsible for defining. The target areas, according to the Department of Education and Science's criteria, were characterised by low economic and social status of parents, poor amenities in the home, high demand for free school meals and large numbers of children with linguistic problems. Educational standards were to be raised by attempts to compensate for the children's inadequate home background and 'positive discrimination' was the key. Five projects were established in Deptford, Balsall Heath/Sparkbrook

Help for the education machine: 'language enrichment' at Deptford EPA, 1971

(Birmingham), Conisborough/Denaby (West Riding), Liverpool 8 and Dundee. Together they cost £175,000, paid jointly by the Department of Education and Science and the Social Science Research Council. The research was co-ordinated by A.H. Halsey who established the Social Evaluation Unit at Oxford for the purpose, and the experiment ran from 1968 to 1971 with the results being written up into a five volume report.

CDP

In 1969 the Home Office set up its version of 'action research': the National Community Development Project. All the themes we are now familiar with were there — concentration on small pockets of deprivation, immigrants and multiple deprivation — and there were two new ones: improving the efficiency of local government through the co-ordination of services, and encouraging participation; ideas derived respectively from the Seebohm and Skeffington Reports.

'A major experiment in improving the social services for those most in need' announced the press release on the Community Development Project. It continued:

This will be a neighbourhood-based experiment aimed at finding new ways of meeting the needs of people living in areas of high social deprivation; by bringing together the work of all the social services under the leadership of a special project team and also by tapping resources of self help and mutual help which may exist among the people in the neighbourhoods.
Home Office Press Release 16.7.69

The twelve Community Development Projects were established, each with an action and a research team, first in Coventry, Liverpool, Southwark and Glyncorrwg and then in Batley, Birmingham, Canning Town, Cumbria, Newcastle, Oldham, Paisley and Tynemouth. The projects were to operate for five years, and cost an estimated £5m in all. There was a strong emphasis on the partnership between government and local authorities, and the Home Office (or Scottish Office in Paisley's case) contributed 75% of the money to the local authorities' 25%. The action teams were to be employed by the local authority and be responsible to a council management committee on which the Home Office was also represented while the research teams were to be 100% financed by the Home Office and based in universities and polytechnics. Their job was to provide a 'diagnosis' of local problems, help generate policy recommendations and evaluate the work of the action team.

Derek Morrell, architect of CDP

The prime mover behind CDP was a civil servant, Derek Morrell — who worked in the Childrens Department at the Home Office, and had previously been at the Department of Education and Science where he had been involved in setting up the Schools Council. This report of his contribution to a meeting held in Coventry in 1969 gives an indication of how he saw CDP:

The whole project is aimed against fragmentation . . . The starting point of the project is that ours is a fragmented, disintegrating society. But the project aims at evolutionary changes, not revolution. Depersonalisation is another problem. The technical juggernaut is taking over and we are no longer the masters. The most difficult step will be how to discover how to perform the crucial task of raising the people of Hillfields from a fatalistic dependence on 'the council' to self-sufficiency and independence
Minutes, 14.7.69

A Tory Government and four more schemes

1970 was election year and no new programmes were initiated. A Tory Government took over and during the three and a half years of their administration new programmes proliferated. In 1971 a new department — the Community Programmes Department — was set up to administer the programmes for which the Home Office was responsible. These included the Community Relations Commission and research projects relating to immigrants, Urban Aid and CDP.

NEIGHBOURHOOD SCHEMES

One of the first projects launched by the Community Programmes Department was the Neighbourhood Schemes, a 'parallel and cross fertilising experiment' for CDP. Unlike Urban Aid which spread relatively small amounts of money over a wide range of projects and areas, these schemes tried the reverse, concentrating a large amount of money into a limited number of areas. The purpose was stated as:

a. to observe and test the effects of co-ordinating £150,000 worth of capital resources going into an area of special social need;
b. to see if this injection of resources could be co-ordinated with local authority resources as a co-ordinated 'social plan';
c. to see how far this could be tied up with area action plans, and, more generally, to see if environmental and social planning could be brought closer together;
d. to act as a laboratory for CDP ideas as they develop;
e. to learn more about how voluntary organisations fit in.
Quoted in CES RP 19 *The Neighbourhood Scheme:* November 197

The emphasis on intensive action in one area and the co-ordination of services coincided with earlier thinking, but there was to be no 'participation' element and a far greater interest in physical rather than social planning. Eventually there were to be ten schemes, but only two were ever set up one in Liverpool (Brunswick) and one on Teeside (Newport). Each scheme was to cost £150,000 in all, paid for directly from the Urban Aid budget, with local authorities making a further financial contribution. All expenditure was for capital projects, with no money for running costs, and all the buildings had to be completed by March 1973.

SIX TOWNS

Shortly afterwards the Department of the Environment announced its own 'total approach' scheme: the Six Towns Studies.

In our approach to the environment, we have endeavoured in the first two years under the new DoE to make a switch of resources to bad areas . . . I believe that the next most important step for my department is to bring about a total approach to the urban problem. In the past the attitude has been a series of fragmented decisions not properly co-ordinated and not bringing about the improvement of urban areas which is necessary.

Peter Walker, then Secretary of State for the Environment, in the Budget Debate 1972, quoted in *Community Action* No.8.

URBAN GUIDELINES AND THE INNER AREA STUDIES

The first three of the 'six town studies', later known as the Urban Guidelines Studies, were located in Oldham, Rotherham and Sunderland. They were undertaken by private management and economic planning consultants and produced reports in the summer of 1973, six months before the local government reorganisation of April 1974. Much of their concern was directed towards how the new local authorities could best deal with urban problems within their areas and particularly the role of councillors within the new structures. All three reports were concerned with improving information flows between the public and the local authority, and improving the co-ordination within and between local authorities.

The second half of the 'six towns studies', the Inner Area Studies, were also undertaken by consultants, but, like EPA and CDP, were action-research projects. The consultants' fees were paid for by the Department of Environment but the local authorities contributed 25% towards the action projects. These three studies were located in Small Heath, Birmingham, Stockwell in South London, and Liverpool 8. They were to

(i)   define inner areas and their problems;
(ii)   investigate, by experiment, actions which could usefully be undertaken for social and environmental purposes;
(iii) examine the concept of area management and its practical implications for local authorities;
(iv) provide a base for general conclusions on statutory powers, finance and resources, and techniques. – Liverpool 1 AS,

Liverpool IAS, *Fourth Study Review,* April 1976.

The studies were well resourced, costing £1.3m so far, and the Department of the Environment clearly attached considerable importance to them. Their wide-ranging brief, as well as their 'action-research' approach, made the Inner Area Studies look very like CDPs, with the use of consultants being perhaps the most important difference.

TRANSMITTED DEPRIVATION

At about the same time as the Department of the Environment was setting up the Six Towns Studies, yet another government department was getting into deprivation'. This time it was the Department of Health and Social Security and Sir Keith Joseph, its Minister, now set up a working party to explore 'whether the cycle of transmitted deprivation would be a fruitful area of research'. In his speech to the Pre-School Playgroups Association in June 1972 he gave a clear picture of his own views:

Why is it that, in spite of long periods of full employment and relative prosperity and the improvement of community services since the Second World War, deprivation and problems of maladjustment so conspicuously exist?

For him the answer lay in investigating how 'deprivation' is passed on through the family. On the basis of the working party's report, the Department of Health and Social Security agreed to finance a seven year programme of research administered jointly with the Social Science Research Council. The programme was to cost £½m in all, but did not have any action element. Lacking any overall direction the programme chose to support research in various academic institutions which coincided with the general interests of the working party.

'The recurrence of social problems through successive

Keith Joseph, Tory Minister of Health & Social Services 1972

generations', was the programme's main emphasis but the working party also supported:

studies of such continuities during a person's lifetime. There is a particular interest in people who break out from a potential cycle of either kind, since such research could be helpful in suggesting how to help others break out . . . likewise factors leading to the initiation of a cycle deserve study.
Transmitted Deprivation Study: *Second Report.*

For a short time the idea of the 'cycle of deprivation' held the stage as the explanation for poverty.

THE QUALITY OF LIFE

Yet another initiative came in 1973 in the form of the Quality of Life Studies, courtesy of the Department of the Environment. These projects, set up in Stoke-on-Trent, Sunderland, Clwyd and Dumbarton, were conceived as part of a 'wider government programme to improve the quality of urban living', and aimed

to bridge the gap between recreational and sporting activities on the one hand and cultural and educational on the other, and to encourage fresh thinking and developing an approach to leisure based on the needs of the community as a whole.
Quality of Life Studies Note May 1976

It was the action-research formula once again. In each area a local steering group was established involving both public and voluntary organisations, like local branches of the Arts and Sports Councils. Professional 'animators' were employed to stimulate and develop local activities, but they were to encourage self-help and find new ways of improving amenities and facilities without drawing on local authority reserve funds. Buses for the disabled, canoe-building groups, support for local theatre groups and play activities for children were some of the results. The programme was designed to last for two years at a cost of around £1m with the research element provided by a central research team within the Department of the Environment. The final reports on the schemes are currently being prepared.

Attempts at co-ordination

By 1973, the Treasury was becoming concerned about the number of different schemes sponsored by different government departments. The Urban Aid Programme, EPA, CDP, Neighbourhood Schemes, Urban Guidelines Studies and Inner Area Studies, the Cycle of Poverty and Quality of Life Studies were dotted around all over the country. They all seemed to be covering more or less the same ground, and duplicating expense as well as effort. The Treasury swung into action and ordered An Inter-departmental Study to investigate the possibilities for rationalisation. Shortly afterwards, in November 1973, Robert Carr, then Home Secretary, announced that a new unit would be established inside the Home Office:

Schemes (to tackle urban problems) are going on in many areas, and these have to be intensified. But something else has to be more intensified: we have to bring them together in a more co-ordinated way . . . We need to learn quickly whatever lessons are available

1974: Roy Jenkins, Carr's successor at the Home Office

not only from our own experience but from the experience of other countries. We need to establish priorities between the programmes so that we can strike a balance between them . . . I have set up in the Home Office a special unit which I am calling the *Urban Deprivation Unit.* This is a unique piece of machinery, designed to meet a special need. . . . I see this work as the key to providing a better life for those who live in the cities and also as a way of improving community relations. Although the urban problem is not one which, in itself, centres on race, large numbers of our coloured citizens live in our older cities. Therefore, if we can remove some of the stress and frustration from urban life we shall at the same time be making an important contribution to better race relations.
Hansard, 1.11.73

THE UDU

The new Urban Deprivation Unit was to be headed jointly by Tom Critchley, an Assistant Under-Secretary at the Home Office, and Gordon Wasserman, an economist responsible for the Inter-departmental Study. At the same time an inter-departmental committee on urban deprivation was set up for the first time. Headed by Tom Critchley, it was supposed to bring together the civil servants concerned with urban deprivation programmes. How frequently it met or what conclusions were drawn from its deliberations is unclear.

In February 1974 the Labour Party, initiators of the first deprivation programmes, returned to power. By now EPA had presented its findings and CDP too was beginning to generate a wide range of reports. As he selected his new ministers, Harold Wilson decided to create a new post inside the planning and local government section of the Department of the Environment. The job, Minister of State (Urban Affairs) appeared briefly and was given to Charles Morris. But urban affairs did not warrant ministerial

Alex Lyon, Jenkin's Minister of State

did not agree with the assumption that there *were* small pockets of 'intense urban deprivation' which could be tackled separately from their areas as a whole. Over a year later the Home Office produced a revised scheme: the comprehensive programmes were now to be drawn up for whole local authority areas. Still, the main characteristic of the CCPs remained the same: by now the emphasis on co-ordination of services and policy feedback was familiar and to it was added the previously implicit policy of re-directing existing resources, rather than providing extra funds.

The 'cycle of deprivation' line was clearly being phased out:

... the problems of urban deprivation are such that they cannot be tackled effectively by means of special compensatory programmes of the self-help or community development type, or by particular innovative or experimental projects such as those financed under the Urban Programme, or even by pumping large amounts of new money into small areas through environ-mental or physical improvement schemes ... There is, therefore, no short-cut to dealing with urban deprivation. The strategy which it is intended to develop in the trial runs is based on the proposition that what is required is to direct the major programme and policies of government to those most in need. Decisions about the allocation of scarce resources must obviously be settled through the political process, but new administrative arrangements can help to ensure that political commitments are translated into effective action.
UDU note, 4.9.75

attention for long, and after the second '74 election the post vanished.

Labour's new initiatives: working out priorities

Just before the October election, though, the Urban Deprivation Unit had come up with another idea. This time it was Comprehensive Community Programmes. Alex Lyon, Minister of State in the Home Office under Roy Jenkins, the new Home Secretary, described the new line.

We reckon that over England and Wales as a whole there are probably about 50 areas that qualify as areas of intense urban deprivation and about 40 areas in Scotland. To make those areas suitable places to live in, one has to channel into them huge resources ... It is not a question of providing the extra money on top of the existing programmes. The real question is to find within existing programmes the right order of priority so that money is spent in urban areas of acute need rather than in other areas ... The object of the exercise is ultimately to produce reports on these areas which will indicate what has been done as a result of close co-operation between government, local authority and voluntary agencies and to indicate also what needs to be done and where the gaps are in the existing programmes.
Hansard, 29.7.74

As ever, the initial discussion however, was about pilot projects. Four were planned but these have taken some time to get off the ground, partly because local authorities

The CCP was essentially a management-oriented scheme: 'an integral part of the local authority's budgeting and decision-making cycle, corporate planning system and committee machinery', bringing in other government agencies as well. Every year the scheme would report on 'the form and incidence of deprivation in the population', 'current policies and programmes intended to meet some of the needs', and the 'programme of action'. Bradford, Gateshead, Wandsworth and the Wirral were selected for trial runs in England. Now it seems the trial runs are themselves to have a trial run — in Gateshead — 'to test the practicability of the approach and to develop a frame-work for the development of CCPs in other areas'. The Gateshead CCP is to cost about £30-40,000 a year. Mean-while, the Scottish Office moved rather more quickly and initiated a CCP in Motherwell which started in the summer of 1976. The idea appears to be that when the trial runs have reported a national deprivation strategy will be developed.

GLC DEPRIVED AREAS

The Urban Deprivation Unit has also been involved in sponsoring a number of smaller programmes, among them the Greater London Council's Deprived Areas Project, based in Spitalfields, Tower Hamlets and Hanley Road, Islington. It provides 75% of the funds (£267,000 p.a. for five years). Described as an 'exercise in co-operation between the two tiers of local government in London involving the co-ordination of existing plans and proposals for the deprived areas as well as the initiation of new action', it will on the basis of these 'pilot schemes', develop a strategic policy for deprived areas in London'.

AREA MANAGEMENT

And not to be outdone, shortly after the announcement of CCPs, the Department of the Environment announced the Area Management Trials. The idea for this came from the Inner Area Study in Liverpool, which itself initiated an area management experiment in Liverpool 8. Other authorities had also developed similar programmes to

a. analyse problems, formulate policies, and monitor their effects in a corporate way at an area level;
b. operate services more sensitively to local needs by better evaluating their performance;
c. provide a convenient channel of communication between the council and neighbourhood councils, residents' associations and other groups and individuals;
d. provide a framework in which elected members can relate council policies to local case-work and vice-versa.

DoE Press Release 6.9.74

Unlike other projects, the Trials were not to involve a team of people, but simply an area manager to co-ordinate policies and act as an access point for local groups. As with most of the programmes, the results of the Trials were supposed to contribute to the making of new policies. Six of these schemes were originally planned, but as yet only two, in Dudley and in Haringey, have started. The amount of money involved is only about £25,000 per year: (75% from DoE), just enough for each scheme funded, to cover salaries and overhead costs for the extra staff. The central government contribution is available for four years, after which the local authority itself will be responsible for the total cost.

THE EEC JOINS IN

With the exception of the Cycle of Deprivation Studies, all the projects and programmes have involved both local and central government and stress has been laid on this 'partnership'. Now, the arrangements have been taken a stage further: the EEC is sponsoring its own 'Poverty Programme'. Part of the EEC's broader Social Action Programme, its special concern is with the 'chronically poor':

Quite apart from the measures proposed in this programme to deal with particular aspects and causes of poverty, the Commission recognises that there will still remain problems of chronic poverty which are unacceptable in an advanced society. There is in the Community a neglected minority of chronically poor, such as the unemployed and their families, families on exceptionally low incomes or fatherless families. Because they are unable in many cases to help themselves or to respond to the help being offered them, these groups find themselves trapped in an almost inescapable cycle of poverty. The rehabilitation of these people and their families is primarily the responsibility of the Member States. However, the Commission believes that it can help Member States to identify the problem and methods of solution through pilot studies and experiments involving amongst other social workers, psychiatrists and local guidance experts.

EEC Social Action Programme, S.2/74

Originally the programme was to last for five years but was cut back to two at a cost of one million units of account to the Community in 1975, and 1.1m in 1976. Participating members had to contribute 50% towards the cost of projects in their own country. In Britain the co-ordination of the programme is the responsibility of the Department of Health and Social Security but funding will come from a range of agencies, including other government departments, the Urban Programme, voluntary bodies, and local authorities for different projects. The total cost will be £850,000.

The aims of the EEC programme sound familiar: 'to develop clearer perceptions of a complex problem and pioneer new techniques for tackling it'. No particular guidelines are laid down for the schemes to be funded other than that 'they cover new ground, are concerned with problems found in more than one country, involve the participation of the poor themselves and a 'multi-disciplinary approach' '. Despite being urged to 'cover new ground' the various projects embody the now very familiar thinking: self-help, participation, surveys of needs, mechanisms for reducing dependence on the welfare services, assistance to socially handicapped families, pre-school compensatory education and co-ordination of services. In Britain there are to be a network of seven family advice centres to help 'the poorest families come to terms with the particular ill effects of extreme poverty'; an area resource centre to help establish self-help groups; a South Wales anti-poverty action centre to provide policy feedback; an area management scheme to ensure participation in resource distribution and a scheme for improving advocacy. Even with such a long tradition of this kind of scheme, the British projects show few advances on the general thinking.

The EEC projects have managed to attract little public attention in Britain. The CCP's and Area Management Trials too were greeted with little of the publicity and attention that the launching of earlier experiments like EPA, CDP or the Inner Area Studies had enjoyed. By 1975 the poverty initiatives were no longer news. The excitment had waned and the focus of attention moved on. To the outside view these inquiries, studies, projects and trials were simply a bewildering mass of different initiatives all coming from different government departments and local authorities all over the country. What logic, if any, links them together is not at all clear. Nor is it clear what there is to show for their efforts or what lessons are to be drawn from this last outburst of state activity on 'urban deprivation'.

SOME RELEVANT GOVERNMENT REPORTS AND WHITE PAPERS

Date set up	reported	Title	Relevant proposal
1956	1960	*Ingleby Report* on Children and Young Persons (Cmnd 1191)	1. need for examination of more co-ordinated family service 2. family advice centres in 'populated areas'.
1957	1960	*Herbert Commission* on Local Government in Greater London (Cmnd 1164)	Setting up GLC to produce co-ordinated local authority for London.
1963	1965	*Milner Holland Report* on Housing in Greater London (Cmnd 2605)	Areas of special control when bad housing can be attacked comprehensively.
—	1965	Future of Development Plans (PAG)	1. new town development plan procedures 2. more public participation.
—	1965	*Children, Family and the Young Offender* (HO Cmnd 2742)	1. set up Seebohm Committee 2. more flexible juvenile courts aimed at involving family.
—	1968	*Children in Trouble* (HO Cmnd 3601)	1. Development Group in Home Office Children's Department
1963	1966	*Plowden Report,* Children and their Primary Schools	Positive discrimination to EPA primary schools
1964	1967	*Maud Committee* on Management of Local Government	More division into decision making and administrative with officials controlling latter. Theory of local authority management.
1964	1967	*Mallaby Committee* on Staffing in Local Government	
1966	1968	*Seebohm Committee* on Local Authority and Allied Personal Social Services (Cmnd 3703)	1. unified social services departments 2. designation of areas of special need.
—	1969	*Skeffington Report* on People and Planning	1. public participation 2. Community Development Officers
1966	1969	*Redcliffe-Maud Report* on Local Government in England. Cmnd 4039/4040	New unitary authorities.
—	1971	Local Government in England (government proposals) Cmnd 4584	Redcliffe-Maud revised.
—	1971	Government proposals for Water (DoE)	New water authorities
—	1971	Local Government Finance (Cmnd 4741)	Arrangements to go with reorganisation.
1971	1972	*Bains Report* — The New Local Authorities Management and Structure	
—	1972	NHS Reorganisation (Cmnd 5055)	New health authorities.
—	1973	*Ogden Report* on New Water Industry	Management arrangements for water authorities.

2 The eradication of poverty?

In terms of government spending this collection of projects and programmes has in fact been marginal. Altogether the various programmes have probably not cost the government more than £10m in any one year since 1968. Yet if you asked a government spokesman what was being done about urban deprivation it is this range of projects, that he would point to. He would claim that although they cost very little, the programmes were intended to have a 'multiplier effect': ideas generated would be taken up by other government departments, local authorities, and voluntary bodies. But did they succeed? Was there an improvement in the situation of people living in these 'areas of deprivation'?

A straightforward answer is difficult to provide. Government statistics are not supplied for such precise purposes, and the most recent census material only covers the period up to 1971. It is not even possible to give an accurate picture for all twelve CDP areas. But a look at the case of Liverpool, a city which has been a testbed for a surprising number of the state's experiments, perhaps begins to give a clearer idea of their effectiveness.

Inside the pockets

The inner city areas of Liverpool are the delight of every deprivation theorist. They have been treated with each of the government's urban deprivation programmes in turn, sometimes with several at a time. An EPA in 1969, a CDP in 1970, a Neighbourhood Scheme in 1971, an Inner Area Study in 1973 which then sponsored an Area Management experiment have all been tried there, and up to 1974 £1,707,213 had been spent on a stunning total of 146 different Urban Aid projects.

According to the Sunday glossies and official reports, Liverpool's inner city is famous for the Kop, empty docks, slum houses and the new catholic cathedral, in that order. Over the last decade it has consolidated its reputation as a place of high unemployment, dereliction and violence. The government-sponsored projects drafted in have all argued that increased job opportunities, increased pre-school education and more spending on housing are essential if anything is to change. What then has been the result? With more money and more projects applied to the area than anywhere else outside London, has the situation for the working-class people of Liverpool's declining areas improved?

In 1968 when the poverty initiatives came to town, 25,000 people were registered as out of work on Merseyside. Four years later their numbers had more than doubled with 52,000 people unemployed. Today, 85,600 men and women, 11.3% of Merseyside's population, are out of work. Even these telling city-wide figures cover up the real story of the inner-city areas. There the predicament of would-be workers is even worse with up to 20% unemployed and up to 30% among younger people.

Left **Battersea, 1962.** *Below,* **Ferguslie Park, Paisley, 1976.**
Overleaf: **Liverpool, 1976. What kind of change?**

One of the most positive recommendations to come out of EPA was the importance of pre-school education. But since 1969 Liverpool has built no new nursery schools. Instead there has been a programme of nursery units attached to primary schools which, by 1976, had provided for less than 5% of the potential need. Further nursery units are under construction or planned, but, like several other EPA innovations, these have been devastatingly cut back recently in response to government-imposed expenditure restrictions. In the primary schools the drop in the number of children in attendance by almost 10,000 since 1969 has not meant significant reductions in class sizes. Instead teacher employment has been cut back in proportion to the declining school population.

Both the CDP and the Inner Area Study agreed that immediate action was needed to tackle inner-Liverpool's housing crisis. But though the message of their reports became more insistent, the actual housing output declined. In 1972 and 1973 the council was completing about 2,500 new houses a year and in 1973 it paid out 9,800 grants for improving older houses. By 1975 only 1,845 new houses a year were being completed and only 2,280 improvement grants were made available. Taking the January to March figures for 1976 it is clear that the situation is even worse: only half that number of houses will be built or improved in 1976. Meanwhile conditions continue to deteriorate.

The poverty initiatives then have clearly not made any great inroads on inner-Liverpool's real material problems. All they have done is to restate, usually in academic terms, what the people who live there have known for a long time. If you live on Merseyside you have a better than average chance of being made redundant, being on the dole for a long time, living in slum conditions, being evicted, and forced to wait over six months for hospital treatment. Your children are more likely to die in infancy, or when, after getting no nursery schooling, they finally get to school, of being in larger classes in worse buildings, only to emerge finally onto the dole. Over 10,000 people leave Liverpool each year as a way of avoiding these problems. Those who are left can debate them in the neighbourhood councils and area management experiments left behind by the 'poverty projects'. But, as they well know, talk is not going to make any impact on the worsening situation that faces them.

The national score

Even if the Liverpool case is conceded, it could still be and sometimes is argued that Liverpool is a special case, unrepresentative of what is going on in other similar areas and in the rest of the country. Nationally there does at first appear to have been some change for the better. In housing conditions, for example, the overall situation seems to have improved. The number of households without basic amenities has decreased rapidly, as predominantly labour authorities honoured their post-war pledges and cleaned out the worst areas of the cities with the massive slum clearance programmes of the mid-sixties. Between 1966 and 1971, for instance, the number of households without hot water was almost halved, dropping from 12.5% to 6.5%. But a closer look at the figures reveals less cause for congratulation.

Although there are now fewer slum tenements and houses in bad condition, and although those people who have a home are more likely to be living in a new one, there are now actually far more people without a home at all. Homelessness has doubled since 1970. On an average day in that year there were 12,874 people applying for temporary accommodation throughout Britain: by 1975 this had increased to 25,120 people a day. Meanwhile there are one million households still on local authority housing waiting lists throughout England while in London alone the total number on the housing waiting list increased from 152,000 in 1965 to 233,000 in 1974.

National unemployment rates show a similar pattern to Liverpool's. Between 1966 and 1971 the numbers of people registered as out of work rose from 1.5% of the adult working population to 3.4%. Now in 1977 it stands at over 6%, with one and a half million people unemployed. For those employed in low-paid jobs many of them living in the inner-city areas, there has been no real improvement in wage levels. In 1964 the poorest 10% of male manual workers earned 71.6% of average (median) earnings. By 1974 this figure had dipped to 68.6%, exactly the same as in 1896. Nor were things any better for the unemployed and sick. In 1967 the supplementary benefit ordinary scale

rates were equivalent to 20.1% of a male manual worker's average weekly earnings. But this was the highest it ever reached: by 1975 the figure had dropped to 17.5%.

Government policy generally, and specifically the poverty initiatives with their talk of 'positive discrimination' has implied progressive redistribution in favour of the less wealthy. Yet the evidence, however difficult it is to assess, does not suggest this has happened to any significant extent. According to the Diamond Commission on the Distribution of Income and Wealth, in 1964 the richest 10% of the population received 29.1% of the country's after-tax income while in 1972-3 the figure was still 26.9%. By contrast the poorest 20% only increased their income during this period from 5.2% to 5.8%. Moreover the wealth statistics show even greater inequalities, with the richest 10% of the population owning 73.5% of the country's wealth in 1965 and 71.9% in 1972-3.

Policy change

The problems of 'deprivation' then would seem to be as acute as ever for those who live them, and the prospects are bleak. Neither the poverty initiatives, nor the government's more general policies towards the poor could be said to have had much impact on the problems facing the people who live in the older urban areas. But the programmes have always been small compared to the size of these. Not so much geared to solving the problems, they set out to provide the basis on which policy at both central and local government levels could be improved. Did the EPAs, Inner Area Studies, CDPs and the rest at least succeed in this respect?

When it came to it neither Tory nor Labour governments seem to have taken much notice of the major policy recommendations emerging from the programmes although several years have now passed since their first reports were available.

More jobs?

Almost all the CDPs and Inner Area Studies have stressed the need to stop the decline of manufacturing industry if any impact is to be made on unemployment and low wages in the older areas. But the Government has rigidly maintained that its existing regional and fiscal policies are the best way to promote industrial growth and relieve unemployment.

Thomas Calton School, South London. Now public spending cuts have finally put paid to plans for new buildings.

Better schools?

The Educational Priority Area schemes reported a wide range of findings on home-school relationships, teaching methods and so on. Underlying all of these were two basic recommendations: more nursery classes and reduced teacher pupil ratios were essential for children in declining urban areas. At first the recommendations seemed to be having some effect: a number of nursery classes were built with money from Urban Aid and in 1972 Margaret Thatcher announced a new programme of nursery class building. By 1976, however, this initiative appears to have been strangled. In 1977-78 government expenditure on building new nursery schools is to be more than halved: whereas the state spent £31.9m on nurseries in 1975-6, in 1978 it plans to spend only £6m. Meanwhile, in many inner-urban areas the number of children of school age is falling. Instead of using the opportunity to decrease the size of their long-overcrowded classes, local authorities are boarding up classrooms and abolishing large numbers of teaching post at a time when thousands of teachers are unemployed.

Better houses?

In housing too the pattern is much the same. One of the major recommendations of all three Inner Area Studies was the need for more spending on house improvement, with changes in policy to allow poorer owner-occupiers to take up improvement grants and more powers to enable local authorities to ensure that rented property was improved. The local authorities got their greater powers in 1974, as part of the Housing Action Areas scheme, but powers alone are useless without money, and they have now been denied the resources to carry out these proposals at all as government spending on improvement grants has gradually been cut back from £195.2m in 1973-4 to £85.8m in 1975-6.

More money?

Why then has the government failed to respond positively to the policy recommendations of its own projects? At a fairly straightforward level the whole issue can be boiled down to a question of resources. The one recommendation that unites all the reports is the need for increased public investment. Plowden, for instance, had reported that 'these neighbourhoods have been starved of new schools, new houses and new investment of every kind. Everyone knows this but for year after year priority has been given to the new towns and new suburbs', and that 'what these deprived areas need are perfectly normal, good primary schools'. The Seebohm Report took a similar view:

Since resources will be relatively scarce in relation to needs however much they are expanded in absolute terms, it seems sensible to concentrate on areas of greatest need. However we do not contemplate that be done by diversion from other areas, thus reducing standards of provision, we expect *additional* new resources to be allocated in a way which gives preference to the deprived and depressed areas.
The Seebohm Report.

Even Roy Jenkins who as Home Secretary was later to take charge of many of the poverty initiatives, said in a book he

Improvement in Saltley: but with the costs far above the levels of grant (even where these are available) few can afford to take up the offer without running into debt.

wrote in 1972:

> There is no simple remedy for poverty. But it could be massively attacked if we carry through certain policies . . . substantial spending *will be required* . . . [his emphasis]
> *What Matters Now.* Roy Jenkins.

and he went on to recommend, among other measures, an eightfold increase in spending on the urban programme.

Yet nothing happened, and the likelihood of it happening now becomes even more remote with the present cuts in public expenditure. Instead emphasis has been given to how what resources there are can be better managed and reallocated, as the two most recent poverty programmes, the Comprehensive Community Programmes and the Area Management Trials, show. Both are designed to find ways of managing urban problems more effectively, not by changing policy but by determining who or what services have highest priority. This is a far cry indeed from Seebohm's insistence that: 'concentration upon priority areas is not in our view an alternative to extra resources — it assumes their existence.'

The new wave

Now during 1976 there has been the new burst of official interest in the 'urban problem'. A good thing perhaps since things are evidently getting no better for the people of the older urban areas. Yet at the same time government policies are making the situation worse. With its current strategy for tackling the national economic crisis leaning heavily on public spending cuts it is once again hitting these areas hardest. Not only are the cuts leading to further unemployment — in construction and manufacturing as well as the public sector — but these cuts mean a severe reduction in the health, education and welfare services on which the poorest in particular depend. While the most recent of the poverty initiatives have abandoned social action for administrative juggling of priorities, the politicians and the media start again to discover the crisis of the city and lobby for action.

But the rhetoric has changed. This time the important problem of industrial change familiar from many of the Inner Area Study and CDP reports has also emerged in both government and opposition statements.

> . . . just as we are all now aware that the future of the nation is inextricably bound up with the fortunes of our manufacturing industries, so too is the future — and the wealth — of the inner areas. We shall need to see what can be done to stem the tide of manufacturing jobs moving out, and the possibility of reversing it.
> *Peter Shore* 17.9.76

The shift of emphasis and the increased concern no doubt reflects the work of the inter departmental committee on deprivation set up in the summer of 1975 (at the same time as the first major cuts in public expenditure). This involved all the departments on the old Critchley Committee, but this time at a higher level of seniority. The committee has sponsored several working groups and will undoubtedly shape what action, if any, is now taken. It is likely for example that serious consideration is being given to the idea of 'New Town Corporations for the inner city areas' and at the very least, it seem probable that several of the existing area management projects will be asked to experiment with some additional resources. It is even possible, now that it has become respectable to help industry at the expense of our social priorities, that inner-city firms will be given grants or financial incentives.

A wider question

But though the industrial change theme has been taken up this was by no means the only issue raised by the last round of poverty initiatives. Most of their reports have gone beyond the demands made in Plowden and Seebohm, and raised more complicated and contentious issues concerning the operation of the existing political and economic system. They are hinted at in this quote from the Liverpool Inner Area Study:

> A number of issues emerge from this description of inner area characteristics and the work carried out by Inner Area Studies. The chief one is the poverty and neglect of the area and its people in every sense. To a great extent this poverty is a reflection of inequalities in society as a whole. Clearly the scale and character of the problem is too great for policies concerned solely and specifically with inner areas to be effective. Any fundamental change must come through policies concerned with the distribution of wealth and the allocation of resources.
> *IAS/L1/6 Third Study Review*, Nov. 1974.

It is in this wider political and economic context that explanations of the government's policies on urban deprivation both now or in the sixties are to be found. For in such a context the poverty initiatives of the late sixties, despite their apparent incoherence and inappropriateness, do have a pattern and logic. To begin to find their real objectives it is necessary to start by looking more closely at what was happening in the wider economy of the time. For it was economic change and industrial reorganisation in particular that was causing the transformation of the older urban areas where the poverty initiatives were set up.

With the urban crisis currently being rediscovered and the likelihood of new government moves to deal with it being introduced, it becomes all the more necessary to understand how and why urban problems suddenly came to the fore in the mid 1960s, and how when the earlier programmes so clearly failed in their apparent objectives such ideas can be enjoying such a vigorous revival today. The rest of this report sets out to offer a few ideas, beginning with a look at the economic background to the changes that were sweeping through the older urban areas and to government activities in the sixties.

Part two
Change in the sixties

3 The problems of capital

'BET YOU, I CAN FOOL ALL THE PEOPLE ALL THE TIME

The 1950s was apparently the decade in which Britain 'never had it so good ', but beneath the tinsel of the post-war boom, there were plenty of signs to show that the economy was vulnerable and uncompetitive in world markets. The growth rate in Britain was slower than in most other industrialised countries. Industry was chronically under-invested, particularly in sectors like the capital goods industries, and output was low. Between 1955 and 1960 for instance the output for all industries and services grew by only 2.5% a year while producitivity (output per employee) rose by only 1.7%.

At an international level on the other hand, there was dramatic expansion in direct investment overseas. Multinational companies, especially American ones, became the dominant force in world trade. With improved communications and transport, they were enjoying a new age in which the large multinationals were able to control the detailed programmes of subsidiaries in every part of the world, switching investment from country to country, and from sector to sector to suit their pockets regardless of the needs of any particular national economy.

Back in Britain, all these factors contributed to a serious decline in the rate of profit. The situation not only threatened the vital process of accumulation essential for

private industry, it also meant that the government was concerned there wouldn't be resources for it to maintain the welfare state at the levels that had come to be expected.

Early in the sixties it became obvious that industry would have to find ways of increasing investment and improving producitivity if it was to survive on the basis of private profitability. The process that followed, had dire consequences particularly for the older urban areas and these together with a full account of what happened are analysed in detail in the CDP report *The Costs of Industrial Change.*

The state to the rescue

Since the war governments had already begun to play an increasing role in the organisation of production, to ensure the survival of private industry. Whole industries like coal, power and the railways, on which all the other industries depended, had been nationalised, and general measures had been brought in to control consumption and demand in a way which was intended to iron out the booms and slumps. But these alone were not proving a sufficient prop: it became clear that the state was going to have to intervene further in the economy.

National planning and more intervention was not of course new to the Labour Party, but in the sixties it became an essential ingredient of economic policy that no government could ignore. Harold Wilson, for instance, argued that only by 'steady industrial expansion . . . by purposive economic planning . . . can we restore our place in the world' — a view echoed in the manifesto on which the Labour Party came to power in 1964.

They [the solutions] will only be achieved by a deliberate and massive effort to modernise the economy: to change its structure and to develop with all possible speed the advanced technology and the new science-based industries with which our future lies.
Lets go with Labour for the new Britain, 1964.

The most ambitious feature of Labour's programme was its National Plan which covered

all aspects of the country's economic development for the next five years . . . Prepared in the fullest consultation with industry, the plan for the first time represents a statement of government policy and a commitment to action by the government.
The National Plan, September 1965.

The basic idea was to induce industry to re-equip with modernised machinery and new techniques, but only nine months after it appeared the Plan was abandoned as a worsening balance of payments problem drove the government to introduce harsh deflationary measures. New private investment was not happening on the scale that was needed and without powers to control the decisions of private industry there was nothing the government could do to alter the situation. What they could and did do was invest more in the public sector and this they did steadily until 1968.

Although therefore the government's direct influence over the investment decisions of private industry turned out to be negligible, it clearly believed that the country's growth depended upon healthy prospects for private profitability: if something could be done about the falling rate of profit, then the problem of how to increase investment might sort itself out. As a fiscal measure, the government introduced Corporation Tax, effectively cutting the amount of tax business and industry had to pay on undistributed profits.

Raising productivity

At company and plant level the crucial issue was productivity. If profitability was to be restored either workers had to be persuaded to produce more for wages that did not increase proportionately, or the number of jobs would have to be cut. Many industries were being substantially reorganised and the result was factory closures, relocation programmes and speeded-up assembly lines. For the workers there were redundancies on the one hand and on the other productivity agreements. The Esso Fawley oil refinery deal in 1964 was one of the earliest of these offering large wage increases in return for specific

changes in working practices. Whereas before 1966 less than half a million workers were covered by productivity deals, the numbers increased by 1,145,000 in 1967, a further three and a quarter million the following year, and by three and three-quarter million more in 1969.

The Wilson administration enthusiatically set about helping this process on its way and introduced a whole range of measures along these lines. To prevent wages rising in step with productivity and to keep down costs for industry, it set up the National Board for Prices and Incomes. It also introduced an initial voluntary wage restraint system which was later replaced in 1966 by successive policies of total freeze on prices and incomes, zero growth and ceilings of 2½-4½% on wage rises. The trade unions also came under scrutiny. The Donovan Commission sat considering them from 1965-68 and paid particular attention to the current system of wage bargaining at factory level between shop stewards and management. To overcome the problems of control this independent local activity had posed for both industry and the national unions its report recommended that 'collective bargaining machinery' should be set up and conditions of employment standardised through an official 'Industrial Relations Commission'. A spate of white papers based on the Donovan recommendations began in the late 1960s and continues to the present day. Advances were made: contracts of employment, closed shops and union activity at the workplace were given legal status, health and safety regulations were tightened up and the unions were allowed limited access to company accounts. At the administrative level, representation of trades unions on

---

Productivity drive for industry

A British Productivity Council campaign to widen the knowledge within industry of techniques for increasing productivity is launched today with a letter to the chief executives of 7,000 medium-sized industrial firms from the Minister for Economic Affairs, Mr. Michael Stewart.

He writes as chairman of the National Economic Development Council and with his letter he has enclosed a pamphlet produced by the British Productivity Council called "Spreading Ideas to Raise Productivity".

January 1967, industry, the state and a mutual concern

economic planning bodies increased rapidly during the sixties, with the first National Economic Development Council set up by the Tories in 1962 and the subsequent Labour Government following with similar councils at the regional level and in certain industries as well. Their greater legal strength not only brought the central union organisations increased status but enshrined it in the official structures of law and government. Top level consultation was formalised and with it came greater control over local trade union activity.

Reorganising industry

The reorganisation of industry in the interests of profitability was happening on a wide scale. This was a reorganisation which would not only enable firms to achieve economies of scale but also make it possible for them to replace workers with machines by introducing new technology. Yet however desirable this might be, for many companies it would cost far more than they were able or prepared to spend. Here too the state could be of some use.

In 1966, the government formed the Industrial Reorganisation Corporation (IRC). By offering industrialists rapid and flexible funding it hoped to persuade top management to push through increases of productivity at company and plant level by rationalisation and merger.

Among the mergers that followed were English Electric-Elliott Automation and AEI-GEC in the electronics industry and the Rootes Motors-Chrysler, and British Motor Holdings-Leyland Motors mergers in the car industry. The overall growth in mergers over this period was substantial as the table below shows, (although the figures for 1967 and 1968 are somewhat distorted by four very large mergers which took place in these years).

Numbers of mergers 1958-68

	Total mergers per annum			Avg. value of net assets transferred: all industry
	Manftg. industry	Distribution & services	All industry	Constant values: £m
1958-60	55	13	68	2.9
1961-63	51	18	69	2.8
1964-65	47	12	59	2.5
1966	48	18	66	3.7
1967	61	14	75	5.1
1968	79	21	100	6.0

To encourage the labour 'shake out' and weaken workers' and trade unions' resistance to the loss of jobs, the government introduced two important schemes, the Redundancy Payments Act (1965) and the earnings-related supplements to unemployment benefit. Presented as part of Labour's general programme of 'technical change tempered with humanity', as Harold Wilson put it, the proposals were clearly viewed as an important device

for restructuring the labour force, and had considerable success. In the first year of the Redundancy Payments Act, £137,000 was paid out and by the year ending September 1969 this form of compensation was running at the £¼m mark. It is true that there was a significant increase in the number of strikes and days lost from 1967 onwards but the vast majority were strikes over wages and conditions, rather than opposition to rationalisation and unemployment. It was not until the Upper Clyde Shipyard occupation in 1971 that workers' resistance to redundancies reached any scale.

The labour shake-out

This policy of rationalisation did appear in the first instance to be having the desired effect. Although the growth of output in the period 1966-71 slackened in almost every sector, there was an average annual productivity increase of 3.4% for all industries and services — a considerable improvement on the previous ten years.

Trends in output and productivity 1955-73
(per cent changes per annum)

	Output			
	1955-60	1960-65	1966-71	1971-73
All industries and services	2.5	3.1	2.2	4.1

	Output per employee (productivity)			
	1955-60	1960-65	1966-71	1971-73
All industries and services	1.7	2.0	3.4	2.8

Source: National Income and Expenditure 1963-73, *Department of Employment Gazette,* British Labour Statistics Historical Abstract, NIESR.

Partly because of external factors like the balance of payments deficit, however, the results were not as dramatic as expected and they proved shortlived. After 1971 growth in the economy levelled off and the increase in productivity began to fall away again.

The idea behind these policies of the sixties was that the workers shaken out of the older industries would be re-employed by other industries which would by this time be growing within the expanding economy. This notion of redistributing workers, or manpower planning, though never developed systematically was reflected in that series of educational reports of the time — Crowther (1959), Newsome (1963), Robbins (1963) and Plowden (1966). But by the end of the 1960s these policies had become increasingly inappropriate. Rationalisation was bringing not more jobs, but a general labour shake-out with redundancies and unemployment rising sharply.

In the nationalised industries, where the state had far greater control, the process was even more extreme. Unlike the private sector, investment *was* substantially increased, opening the way for extensive rationalisation and increasingly sophisticated management techniques.

Far from benefiting the labour force this only made things worse faster. The nationalised industries became far more 'economically sound', but an even higher proportion of jobs were lost than in the private sector. In British Rail and the National Coal Board alone, 700,000 jobs disappeared in the period between 1960 and 1975. Many of these were in areas where a single industry dominated local employment. In these places no amount of manpower planning could prevent rationalisation from producing high unemployment.

Capital's state

The sixties then were years of rapid industrial change, in which the government facilitated the decisions of private enterprise. There were examples, as with the Industrial Reorganisation Corporation, where government intervention may well have accelerated trends in particular industries, but overall it was the decisions of capital that were shaping the pace and form of industrial reorganisation. Moreover control of these decisions was becoming increasingly concentrated in large multi-national companies, whose prime concern was to find the most profitable outlet for their capital. Thus by the end of the 1960s continuing investment of industrial capital abroad, and the switching of pension and insurance funds into the property market at home was resulting in low rates of investment of new capital in British manufacturing industry. Nor have the 1970s brought any improvement . The rate of private investment has remained low with industry, in the case of Rolls Royce, British Leyland and Chrysler for example, drawing heavily instead on public funds. But though the state may intervene in cases like these to avoid conspicuous numbers of workers becoming unemployed in the same place at the same time, unemployment now at one and a half million threatens to become a permanent part of the economic picture, whether the promised 'regeneration of industry' happens or not.

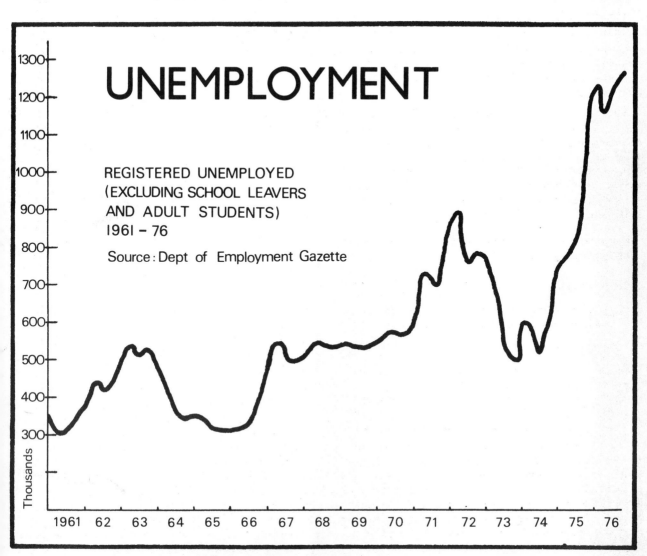

UNEMPLOYMENT

REGISTERED UNEMPLOYED
(EXCLUDING SCHOOL LEAVERS
AND ADULT STUDENTS)
1961 – 76

Source: Dept of Employment Gazette

4 Problems for the working class

There is a general feeling of frustration, a feeling that life has little purpose in such insecure conditions where everyone is threatened with the loss of his job. Most of the old crafts have disappeared, taking away the opportunity once open to workers of acquiring skills or developing creative talent. The young man entering the industry as an unskilled worker will probably remain so for the rest of his life.
The Incompatibles, Robert Doyle

Plant is only one of the factors, however. In Britain today, people are, by and large, enjoying a good standard of living and compared with many countries wages are high (although, of course, not as high as most people would like). Human resources, however, are scarce and expensive and therefore it makes sense to see that they are fully used and not misused. Just as it does not make sense to build more plants before we fully use the ones we have, neither does it make sense to keep on hiring men when some of those we have cannot make a full contribution because of bad organization or working habits.
There are two ways, therefore, in which a company can increase it efficiency:

1. By better use of plant.
2. By better use of people.

One way to achieve these aims is to work plant and equipment more hours either by adding hours on to existing shifts, i.e. overtime or by working different shifts, or by a combination of both. Not everybody understands the reasons behind this.
From *Two Heads are Better than One:* Ford Motor Company Department of Labour Relations.

They say that their timings are based upon what an 'average man' can do at an 'average time of the day'. That's a load of nonsense that. At the beginning of the shift its alright but later on it gets harder. And what if a man feels a bit under the weather? On night shift see, I'm bloody hopeless. I just can't get going on nights. Yet you've always got the same times: Ford's times. It's this numbering again. They think that if they number us and number the job everything is fine.

I came there and I was put on the front of the line. There was all these hooks and they *all* had to be filled with bits and pieces. I tell you Huwie it was murder. I'd get home and I'd go straight to bed. I couldn't stand it. So I decided that I'd had enough I started to fill every other hook — to leave big gaps. The foreman went mad. Berserk he went. He started jumping on and off the line, running down the shop filling up the hooks. I ask you. He was shit-scared. 'You-*must* fill them all' he kept screaming. Well the lads caught on and they started leaving empty hooks. He was going crazy. Then we got hold of Eddie to complain that the foreman was working. We did that every day.

The situation is a lot better now. In fact we've got one of the easiest sections in the plant. It can be done see. You can control it if you have a go.
Working for Ford, Huw Benyon.

The rationalisation and reorganisation of industry in the sixties was a problem for working-class people in almost every community from the East End of London to villages dependent on a single pit in Fife or West Glamorgan. Men were being replaced by machines while new technologies made old skills redundant and put new techniques in their place. Reorganised production processes and method study were 'deskilling' jobs and putting increasing pressure on workers to match targets determined by the capacity of machines. British Leyland, for instance, now admit that ten years work in the factory 'burns people up' and want to halt recruitment of workers over thirty years old.

Paying the price

The pattern of change varies from area to area, and with it the problems facing workers. For those in the more prosperous areas who were able to get jobs, there were still the personal and social problems caused by the monotony of the production line and the increasing use of shift-work. For workers in the older industrial areas there were other factors making things worse. They saw little of industry's new investment. What new plant there was was usually built on the outskirts of cities or in the new towns where transport was good, and cheap land was available for development and expansion. The older areas paid the price. Between 1966 and 1971 manufacturing employment in Manchester declined by 20%, in Liverpool by 19%, in Birmingham by 13%, in Newcastle by 11% and in Inner London by 18%. These statistics of decline for whole cities could be doubled for intensive industrial zones like east Birmingham, the London docks or the Tyne and Mersey waterfronts.

The consequences of the changes were immense. In Canning Town in the East End of London for example, over 17,000 jobs were lost between 1966 and 1972, with almost half of all the area's workers being made redundant at sometime. In East Birmingham there were at least 10,000 redundancies between 1965 and 1975. Unemployment rates in certain areas rose to between 10% and 15%. In Glyncorrwg in 1968 just before the CDP was set up there it touched 33%.

Those who were thrown out of work soon found out how inadequate the local industrial retraining facilities were. There may have been talk of manpower planning at a national level, but it was rarely matched by programmes relevant to local conditions. Skilled workers from the engineering shops and shipyards were forced into low-paid jobs in the service sector or into boring work in new warehouses or the assembly line. Redundancy money soon disappeared once a whole family had to live on it for several months. Those who could, found work within commuting distance of their existing homes. Others, the mobile, the young, those whose skills were still saleable, moved out: to the new towns, to more prosperous areas or even, like others before them in the 1880s and nineties, overseas. The rest were forced to stay where they were, trapped in the wastelands round the collapsing older industries. They were joined by those who could find nowhere else to go.

In some places many of these newcomers were immigrants and they experienced special types of exploitation and humiliation. Encouraged to migrate to Britain in the 'boom' fifties, most found themselves stuck with unskilled, dirty or nightshift work which other city workers had been

Progress for the older areas: blighted housing, Southwark

reluctant to do. They remained in these jobs, which were often poorly paid and poorly unionised. The problems of discrimination, especially in housing, were exploited by sharp estate agents, solicitors and landlords. Those who did find decent places to live were expected to help out their fellow immigrants, often causing overcrowding. Many men with families became enforced batchelors in Britain as the state threw up barriers to prevent their wives and children joining them. The host community of the older areas, many of them the disappointed elderly who had been left behind, were not easy neighbours to please. Misunderstandings were fanned into racialism often by national politicians and the media. Immigrants became scapegoats for the very conditions they themselves most suffered from. In the latest period of high unemployment, the problem has reached levels of 20-30% among black workers, even in the larger cities.

As the industrial shake-out proceeded, the older working-class areas, already faced with widespread unemployment, high transport costs, low wages, the loss of skilled workers, were also affected by physical changes. At last local authorities began to make subtantial, if overdue, efforts to meet working-class demands for better housing. At the same time the large amounts of money being invested in land and urban development were having their effect and like other industries, the big building and engineering firms were using the new investment to develop new production techniques. As the local authority clearance programmes advanced, the nineteenth century slum terraces came down and in their place new systems-built flats and prefabricated tower blocks went up.

For many people this brought the chance of a new and better home, but redevelopment also meant having to live through months and sometimes years of the blight and

Lost jobs, Saltley. British Leyland's Adderley Park Van Plant after rationalisation

dereliction of a demolition area — with all the accompanying problems of declining services, rubbish dumping and rats. In 1975 for instance Birmingham City Council were still rehousing people whose homes had been condemned in the mid-sixties and whose neighbours had been rehoused in the late sixties. At the end of the process the homes they had gained were often not what they wanted and the problems of finding work were just as acute as they had been before.

While the state could afford to allocate resources for expensive redevelopment programmes at times of economic growth, towards the end of the sixties the economic situation was deteriorating. The 1969 and 1974 Housing Acts marked a significant shift in government policy away from redevelopment and towards improving the older houses instead of replacing them. But though the working-class communities that remained intact welcomed these policies, for most it was too late. Blight had taken its toll and this new policy move was by no means a balanced shift in government policy away from the by now unpopular high-rise flats to rehabilitating the same number of older houses. In the context of increasing cutbacks in public expenditure what it in fact amounted to was a fundamental shift of resources away from the provision of working-class housing in the inner city altogether.

With low incomes and often exploitatively high mortgage charges, few owner-occupiers in the older areas could afford to improve their homes, while landlords, reluctant at the best of times to do even basic maintenance like mending the roof, saw little attraction in risking further capital when there were other much safer places, like the building societies, to invest their money.

Resistance

For the individual worker thrown out of a job, or the tenant watching physical neglect push these areas further into decline, there may have seemed little that could be done. But at a wider level it was clear that working-class people were hitting back at the industrial and physical changes that were overtaking them. The reorganisation of industry was being reflected in a reorganisation of working-class struggle.

In the workplace the most significant development was the renewed growth of the shop stewards' movement during the sixties. In part this came from the need to bargain at plant level over the new shift rates, incentive schemes and productivity agreements that were being introduced. But equally significant was its move to bring control of the trade unions away from the central organisations and base it firmly back on the shop floor in the everyday struggle for the control of production. After years of relative inertia this was an important advance and it didn't escape the notice of the government. The Donovan Commission was set up in 1965 to look into how the situation could be brought under control. Though the strength of the sixties shop stewards' movement was mainly directed at improving wages and working conditions, it was the threat of a militant shopfloor movement that largely prompted the Labour Government to introduce the *In place of strife* proposals in 1969. The idea was to control unofficial strikes by law since the central trade unions seemed unable to do the job. These strikes, it implied, were the cause of the country's economic problems. The protest that followed was too great for the Labour Government and, for the time being the proposals were dropped. With their departure, the wave of resistance receded, but it came to a peak again in the fight against the Tory version of the same policy: the Industrial Relations Act of 1972. This marked the culmination of the wage struggles of the sixties. By the seventies the crisis had worsened and with wage control brought in and even accepted, the resistance began to turn against rising unemployment. The early seventies saw direct action by workers trying to preserve their jobs become far more common than before. There were occupations, work-ins and worker co-operatives and these were accompanied by increasing demands from workers for much greater involvement in the management and control of the industries where they worked.

Nor was the struggle confined to the workplace. Housing and community issues may not traditionally have been an area for widespread working-class action, except perhaps around the period of the First World War. The late sixties however saw the mushrooming of large numbers of tenants and action groups protesting about housing programmes, motorway schemes, central area redevelopment. There were rent strikes. There was the rise of squatting on a large-scale for the first time since the war. This growth in community action at a local uncoordinated level reflected a growing concern with the consequences of urban redevelopment, but it was the widely-supported campaign in 1971 against the Tories' Housing Finance Bill and its provisions for increasing rents through the 'fair rents' system that began for the first time to raise the wider class implications of the state's changing housing policy and mobilise resistance on a national scale. Ironically it was summed up best by Anthony Crosland in his attack on the second reading of the bill:

Our basic objections are to the drastic effect it will have on the cost of living, to the spread of means testing ... to the reversion which it implies to one-class welfare housing, and also to the sharp consequent increase in inequality.

Industrial reorganisation in general did mean increased inequality and the workers and residents of the older areas were getting the worst of it, but looked at across the country as a whole it was also bringing increased resistance and new forms of struggle. Though the growth of this resistance may have been largely piecemeal and uncoordinated it could clearly grow very quickly as the campaigns against the Industrial Relations Act and the Housing Finance Bill had shown. As such it not only presented problems for industry but also for the state.

And for the state in particular the situation of the older

working-class areas in decline, now being homed in on by press, social reformers and politicians, presented responsibilities and problems which it had to take up.

From being a problem for the people of these areas, their day to day experience of poverty, exploitation and bad conditions, the older urban areas became a problem of government.

The working class could not be relied upon to agree with either local or central state policies. *Top left:* Liverpool. Council tenants occupy local housing department offices in protest at lack of repairs and improvements. *Below (and cover)* slogans from the 1972 rent strike, Liverpool CDP area.
Bottom left: On a national scale, squatting was spreading, evictions were being resisted, and at the same time there was mounting resistance to central government legislation. *Centre* demonstration against the Housing finance bill

5 The problem for the state

The Oldham CDP area. A potential threat? The 'deprivation' literature was much concerned with disorders of the young

Government and Welfare State were experiencing new strains. For them the problems arising from the developments of the sixties were posed in very different terms to the working-class experience. This indeed was part of the trouble: with the situation of the older areas worsening the credibility of the official version of events was coming into question.

Explaining away

This was after all the mid-twentieth century, supposedly the post-war age of economic stability, firmly based in technological and scientific advance, and logically explained through social science. Not only had we 'never had it so good' but the prospect for the future was greater affluence to be shared by all. Comprehensive education showed the way — inequalities would gradually disappear and class distinction fade away. Expectations were high. Against such a background the continuing presence of poverty could not be ignored. And the fact that poverty was actually increasing threatened to call into question the reality of the 'affluent society'.

So the obvious disparity between the day-to-day experience of working-class people and the generally accepted notion that everyone was enjoying increasing affluence had to be confronted and explained. While heavily involved in maintaining profitability for private industry the state also had to tackle the difficult task of convincing the people that these inequalities would soon disappear. In addition it had to deal with the practical consequences of the industrial change it was promoting.

Keeping the lid on

The changing population structure of the older urban areas had serious implications for the welfare state. For as the economic base of these working-class areas collapsed and the skilled, the mobile and the young moved out, the traditional family and community networks which had previously provided support for local people were badly undermined. For the moment there might be little organised protest about urban conditions but truancy and vandalism were growing. Social studies like Willmot and Young's pioneering *Family and Kinship in East London* (1957) had for some years been indicating that the 'decline in community' was to blame and the Seebohm Report of 1968, voicing a 'concern at the increase in officially recorded delinquency' emphasised 'the need to concentrate resources and a belief that preventative work with families was of cardinal importance in this context'.

The departure of many of the skilled, respectable people who had previously been active in providing organisation and leadership, often through the labour movement, presented other problems too. There was no longer a clearly identifiable structure in the community through which local officials and politicians could keep in touch with what was going on.

An additional problem for them was that in some places large numbers of black immigrants were moving in and becoming the focus of racial tension. But though many of the social studies might speak with genuine liberal concern about the problems and the suffering being experienced by the inhabitants of the declining areas, the problem for the state overall was not their suffering so much as the potential trouble their very existence represented.

There is now a large group of people whose incomes are not sufficient to maintain life without substantial special help. These people depend on means-tested benefits of one kind or another . . . ever increasing tracts of our older cities could be inhabited by such people . . . But if we do allow such a new urban under-class to emerge the consequences will be severe. There will be a permanent housing problem, nomadism, an unstable family life. There could be increased tension especially on an ethnic basis. Dereliction, abandoned old premises, failure to build new property and maintain the old will lead to progressive blight and decay.
Urban Problems in Britain Today, David Eversley, 1972.

British cities were not about to erupt at any moment perhaps, but there were precedents. There had been race riots in Notting Hill in 1958 and in 1967-68 the race riots that had flared up in several cities in the USA resulted not only in many deaths but in extensive damage to property. This same period reflected increasing tensions in Europe — student revolt, strikes and occupations, and demonstrations that centred in the cities and raised political questions about government policy at home and abroad. Britain, too, was affected by the wave of unrest. In May 1968 the pound fell to an all-time low providing a background of economic disquiet. On 6th October the Stormont Government's ban on a civil rights march had triggered street fighting in Derry, and in London 100,000 people marched through the streets in protest at the Vietnam war.

Nor was it just the organised political protesters who were causing concern. There had been mods and rockers and clashes between them, and now the skinheads were hitting the headlines along with other juvenile rebels who were engaged in vandalism and football hooliganism. For the state these outbreaks were not only worrying and difficult to control, they were expensive too.

The Notting Hill riots, 1958

The bottomless pit

The problem wasn't merely explaining the concentrations of poor people in the cities or controlling them by force when they got out of hand. The state was heavily involved in providing support and services in the hard-hit working-class areas, and this too was costing it more and more.

Concentrations of poor people in these areas were putting a great strain on the personal social services and on the social security system. The high unemployment rates, low wages and high proportion of pensioners meant heavy claims on unemployment and social security benefits. The overcrowded houses and concentrations of old people on the one hand and families with young children on the other put an increasing burden on the welfare services. Housing waiting lists were long and getting longer all the time. Individual local and central government officials were under pressure.

The fact that the people who depended most on the Welfare State were concentrated in the worst areas in the country enabled them to be singled out as an easy target. These areas were 'bottomless pits' eating up state resources, as the first CDP press release put it in 1968. It was not just that there was a higher proportion of people in such places eligible for state support but the ways in which they had formerly cared for each other were breaking down, and when family or neighbour support failed they were going to the social services or social security causing further 'expense'.

Unemployed workers put state services in business, but seen from the other side of the counter the poor were just too expensive

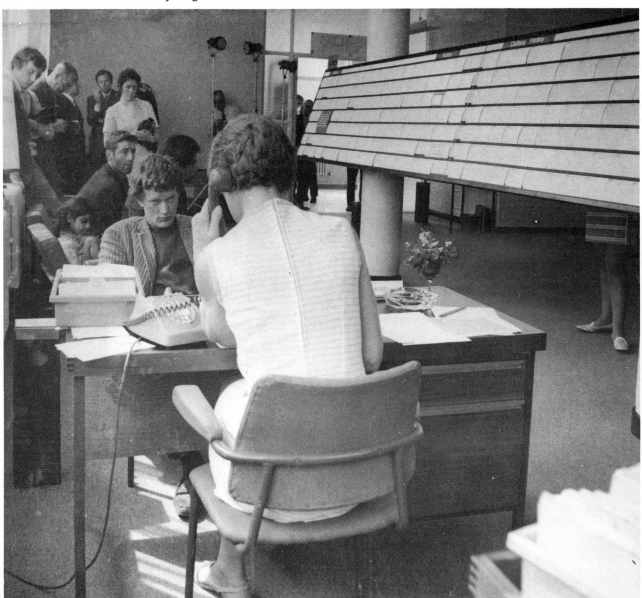

An old problem

The problem of the working class was nothing new to the 1960s. The developing capitalism of the nineteenth century had been even more vicious in neglecting the welfare of its labour force both in work and outside it. But over the intervening years a long struggle waged by the working class had brought into existence improved conditions and a welfare state.

In the early nineteenth century it had been 'charity' and its organisations that dealt with the problem of the poor, but as the industrial revolution precipitated not only new forms of intensified misery for the workers but also increased concern among social enquirers and philanthropists the demand was raised for the state to take over.

There is no more hopeful sign in the Christian Church of today than the increased attention which is being given by it to the poor and outcast classes of society. Of this it has never been wholly neglectful; if it had it would have ceased to be Christian. But it has, as yet, only imperfectly realised and fulfilled its mission to the poor. That something needs to be done for this pitiable out-cast population must be evident to all . . . Despair of success in any such undertaking may paralyse many. We shall be pointed to the fact that without State interference nothing effectual can be accomplished upon any large scale.
The Bitter Cry of Outcast London, Andrew Mearns, 1883.

Then too it was not just a matter of concern for the plight of the poor. Many of these poor were in fact part of a growing working-class movement that was beginning to make its own demands on the government. The Chartist movement and the development first of the craft-based trade unions and later of the unions of casual and unskilled workers in the great strikes of the 1880s reflected growing opposition among the working class to their lack of political representation and appalling conditions.

Right: out of work, into the workhouse. The nineteenth century solution was to punish the destitute for the failure of their employers. But workers rose to their own defence. *Below,* a meeting of gas-workers on Peckham Rye, London during the 1889 strike. The organisation of un-skilled workers like these was a turning point for the state

The making of a welfare state

Gradually the government did become involved in welfare issues. At first it was concerned to protect workers from the worst aspects of exploitation at work, through the Factory Acts but very quickly other aspects of working-class life became the subject of legislation. The 1870s saw a spate of laws to protect the interests of the new working class. There were more factory acts, housing and health legislation, the 1870 Education Act. The state was beginning to respond to the pressure of social reformers, urban misery and its own fears of working-class unrest. But it was undoubtedly acting in the interests of capital too.

If profitable production was to be able to continue in the long term, capital could not afford to ignore the wellbeing of its workers altogether. It was necessary to ensure a continuing supply of labour, the reproduction of new generations of healthy workers on the one hand, while on the other it was essential to keep those workers from open insurrection. There was no evidence that, left to its own devices, nineteenth century capital was either able or willing to meet either of those necessary conditions for its own survival. In the unsanitary squalor of home and factory, workers were being killed and maimed, children were growing up deformed and revolt seemed imminent. So, cued in by horrified social reformers, government stepped in.

The reforms of the 1870s were only the beginning and successive governments found themselves under continuing strong pressure. The turn of the century was a period of intense conflict between workers and the owners of industry. Union leaders were openly talking of the need to change the political and economic system. Lloyd George's Insurance and Health Acts of 1911 which introduced welfare benefits for the first time was a response, in part, to this working-class pressure. The First World War and the Russian Revolution, with the extensive suffering brought by the one and the political alternatives raised by the other, were further spurs to the government to better the conditions of the working class. The 1919 Housing Act for example, which marked the first full-scale national council housing programme, was a consequence of both pre-war legislation over housing conditions and the industrial unrest and rent strikes in Glasgow in 1915. Similarly the widespread unemployment and intense poverty of the 1930s together with the experience of the Second World War led to a fresh spate of welfare legislation in the 1940s.

But in conceding working-class demands to secure the future of capital, the state had not merely reproduced the operations once left to church and charity. As time had passed, the plethora of reforming measures had been steadily rationalised and channelled. New structures and new institutions had been created and though they owed their very existence to working-class pressure and liberal concern, their *form*, the ways in which they were organised and operated, had also been shaped by the state and its needs.

The state reorganises

Over the years there had been a succession of moves to centralise and rationalise the provision of welfare. At first movement was slow, but by the twentieth century the pace had quickened. The National Assurance Act of 1948 marked the culmination of a series of steps which finally replaced the old, locally organised Poor Law system and Boards of Guardians. These had been the subject of widespread attacks by unemployed workers in the 1930s, and now a new unified national structure was introduced independent of direct parliamentary control and free of local political pressures. In 1946, years of working-class pressure finally resulted in the setting up of a free health service with The National Health Service Act bringing the vast majority of former municipal and voluntary hospitals under the control of a co-ordinated regional structure.

If the 1940s saw the establishment of the Welfare State as as we know it today, the fifties and sixties saw it not only grow overall but develop and rationalise itself. Now as the economy was being reorganised the concern inside the state too was for increased efficiency. Local government structures had to be overhauled to allow a more effective response to the needs of the economy, similarly the education system had to be adapted to produce a more flexible workforce capable of meeting the needs of an increasingly fast-changing technology-based economy. It was not only a matter of extending education but of creating new institutions: technical colleges, new universities polytechnics and comprehensive schools. At each stage the issues of the original struggle for the Welfare State emerged again, but they were often disguised as administrative decisions.

The 1960s was a period of great activity amongst civil servants and others drawn in from outside. They not only produced the numerous reports mentioned earlier but endless white papers on how the various services of both central and local government could be improved and reorganised to meet the new pressures. The result was a series of measures which further centralised and co-ordinated the structures and services of government.

In 1966 for example the Police Act reformed the police forces into larger units, at the same time centralising their crime prevention and intelligence functions. In 1969 the Royal Commission on Local Government (The Redcliffe-Maud Report) proposed the total transformation of the local authority structure. Implemented in 1974 it meant that just seven metropolitan counties including the GLC were now responsible for a population of 18.8 million people, 38% of the country's total population. Further education institutions were expanded and upgraded to provide degree courses as well as more liberal education. Many other areas were affected too — bus transport, reorganised under the National Bus Company (1968), town planning (1968), social services (1970) following the Seebohm Report, the system of law courts (1971), the area health authorities (1973) and water authorities (1973).

Bigger and better

The moves to centralisation brought a sharp increase in social spending. Throughout the sixties public and in particular local government expenditure was taking up a higher and higher proportion of total expenditure. With an increasing amount of this money actually being provided by central government, through the Rate Support Grant, the entire field of local authority spending in turn became a target for rationalisation. Integration and co-ordination, at the local level were key themes of the Maud (1967), Seebohm (1968), and Bains (1972) Reports, and were followed by innovations like corporate management and the local authority reorganisation already described. At the same time the government increasingly used the fact that it controlled the Rate Support Grant to exercise control over the actions of local authorities. A recent example is the government's insistence that the GLC and other metropolitan authorities increase bus fares instead of subsidising them through the rates.

One might have anticipated that this move towards undermining the traditional autonomy of local government and further centralising control of its expenditure and activities would have been greeted by members of local councils with some resistance. Indeed there have been some incidents of this kind. The labour councillors of Clay Cross refused to implement the Housing Finance Act in 1972 and the tories of Tameside insisted on throwing out comprehensive education in 1976, both groups of councillors asserting their right to determine policy at a local level on political grounds. Another example is the snub the Association of Municipal Corporations (AMC) gave to the Home Office directive that, in the context of Urban Aid, councils should work closely with the new tenants' and similar organisations that were springing up in the inner city area:

... such groups were not the kind of voluntary body which the Urban Programme should aid. Local Authorities were better able to tell which local voluntary bodies were worth supporting ... *Municipal Review*, November 1973.

In the main, though, these changes were accepted by the local councils. Indeed they had been well represented on the Royal Commissions which had recommended the changes in the first place. They also had a vested interest in making their services more efficient, for it was they who had to answer to the immediate pressures when the movement of investment and jobs created unemployment or changes in the demand for skills in their areas: it was their services which had to provide the relief of the hardship that followed.

The state as problem solver

The rationalisation, reorganisation and centralisation of government had followed a clear pattern with good reason. At first, municipal services from housing to the police had been established wherever the need appeared, in a fairly ad hoc way. But after the Second World War state intervention, whether in the field of 'law and order', social welfare, or industrial policy, no longer confined itself to sorting out crisis situations.

The state came to adopt an increasingly assertive role in the management of the economy as a whole in the interests of restoring private profitability, as well as intervening to encourage particular industries and companies to restructure, and introducing legislation to make their task easier. There was also the massive growth of planning, and the introduction of new, more sophisticated management techniques in local and central government while local and central public expenditure became part of an integrated state function manipulated from the centre. Overall it was clear that the state was now much more concerned with making sure that economic changes would succeed and that they could be carried through effectively without causing too much resentment among the working class. Rather than just responding to immediate pressures the developments of recent years signalled the state gearing up for a far greater problem-solving role.

The process was not merely a one-way growth of centralised government. The development of the state brought a huge expansion of its operations, its cost and the number and variety of workers who made it up. Extending from police and judiciary, from elected members, Whitehall civil service or local government administrators to teachers, social workers, planners, to home helps, street sweepers and hospital ancillary workers, the state spread into all sections of the population.

While any account of the *overall* development and activity tends to make the state appear a single like-minded block it would be a great mistake to see it as a monolith. As the state has extended its tentacles so it has come to include within it, many whose activities were formerly outside, sometimes even against it. Now safely contained within the institutional structures virtually the whole range of classes and opinions, some liberals and radicals included, co-exist as working parts of the same governing structure. Indeed this in itself has been part of the process of constructing the problem-solving face of the state.

[CDPs] are not a means for channelling money into areas of need. They were designed to put teams of articulate young people into areas where the population, though deprived, was inarticulate, to help those people to express their own sense of grievance and to put pressure on the authority to do something about the situation.
Hansard, Alex Lyon, 29.7.74

What has to be remembered though, is that these developments have never been an *explicit* part of the programme of any political party whether in government or in opposition. They may have had a profound effect on every aspect of life but they have never been openly proposed, voted for or even acknowledged as an issue of public politics. Many of them have been administrative decisions, institutional changes, questions of 'management'. The development of the state has proceeded steadily while governments of different hues have come and gone. The historical links of Conservative Party with the interests of industrialists and Labour Party with the working-class movement are mere decoration compared with that steady process.

The state — the apparatus of government which makes sure taxes are paid, children are taught in school, law and order is maintained in the streets and single parent families get

their giro cheques — is constantly being adapted in a similar direction by whichever party is in power.

New face, old role

The changes in the nature and organisation of the state described above should not be mistaken for a change in its basic role. Its areas of activity and the range of its workers may have expanded and certain circumstances may have altered, but its task remains the same and its institutions are governed by that task. As in the nineteenth century it has on the one hand to ensure the continuing profitability of private capital; on the other it has to deal with the consequences of the way that capital operates and ensure that the working class accept these consequences. With the working class both the source of profit for capitalism and the greatest threat to its existence, the state has to be constantly sensitive to working-class demands while at the same time ensuring that any unavoidable concessions interfere as little as possible with the long term interest of capital. Between these two tasks lie the contradictions for the state. And in the 1960s and seventies as always it was these which governed the initiatives of the time.

With possibilities for reform closely linked with economic growth, by 1968 room for manoeuvre was becoming limited. The kind of growth the state had tried to engineer was just not taking place. There were already attacks on rising public expenditure. The first post-war cuts of £700m over two years were made at the beginning of 1968 as part of the government's deflationary policies as it tried to resolve the balance of payments crisis. So the welfare aspect of the state's policy was constrained still further. It was imperative for it to act on the urban problem but it had to do so in a way that wouldn't place any further burden on public spending. New forms and techniques had to be devised to carry out the state's old role. More aggressive problem solving, but within a framework of limited or reduced expenditure had to be the key. Seen in this light the poverty programme takes on a new logic.

November 1966, news of cuts

Cabinet seeking £120M cuts in public spending

By PETER JENKINS

A total of £120 millions is believed to be involved in the Cabinet arguments about cuts in next year's public expenditure.

These are real cuts which Ministers must apply to their cherished programmes if the Chancellor is to prevent the Government's cash expenditure from rising by more than 6 per cent during 1967-68.

Part three
A task of goverment

6 Law and order

The urban problem is fundamental to the problems of our society
and the level of crime in our society . . . The level of crime is only
the visible tip of the iceberg of social ferment lying beneath.
Hansard, Robert Carr (Home Secretary), 1.11.73

Below: the policeman. Visible tip of the State iceberg?

The most obvious of the State's instruments are probably the forces of control: the army, police, prisons and courts. Like the reflection of Robert Carr's image of crime they are the visible tip of the state iceberg. Facing them in the sixties was the old and central problem of government: if capital was to operate smoothly and profitably, a stable society and an orderly and well-disciplined workforce was essential, yet the process of capital development itself was constantly throwing up friction, conflict and violence with which the state had to deal.

The need to adapt to new conditions was recognised. During that decade expenditure on law and order almost doubled as a proportion of total public expenditure. In addition the police force was reorganised and a whole series of official reports gave their attention to one of the more serious issues of the time, the growing level of crime and in particular juvenile crime.

Home Office, the Children's Department was formulating a new approach to preventing juvenile delinquency at source. The resources of the community were to be mobilised both to support the family and to develop a wider sense of responsiblity for keeping children under control. The Report expressed concern about the rapid increase in juvenile delinquency during the 1950s which could no longer be explained by a war situation and therefore could not be expected to die down of its own accord. New ways of coping with the problem had to be devised and the family had to be helped to do its job of bringing up children properly:

The primary responsibility for bringing up children is parental and it is essentially a positive responsibility. It is the parents' duty to help their children to become effective and law abiding citizens by example and training and by providing a stable and secure family background in which they can develop satisfactorily.
The Ingleby Report, 1960.

Expenditure on law and order as a proportion of total public expenditure

1910	1937	1951	1961	1971	1973
0.6	0.7	0.6	0.8	1.3	1.4

Prevention begins at home

It was surprising perhaps that it was the Home Office, the government department responsible for the law enforcement agencies, that initiated most of the early poverty programmes. As well as having the task of co-ordinating the state's activity in relation to immigrants and, up to 1969, controlling the Children's Department which dealt with children in care and policy on the treatment and prevention of juvenile crime, it was now this department that produced first the Community Relations Commission and Urban Aid in 1968 and then CDP (1969); Neighbourhood Schemes (1971) and the Comprehensive Community Programme (1974). It was also a civil servant from the Home Office who chaired the government's high level cabinet advisory committee on urban deprivation up to mid-1975, when the Department of the Environment took over. While all these programmes were avowedly designed to combat various aspects of poverty such as bad housing and dependence on the social services, the Home Office was a department with no responsibility for or control over any of these services. Why then the interest of the Home Office in urban poverty?

The origins of the Community Development Project suggests that its concern was not in poverty itself, but in the consequence of poverty — specifically the rising crime rate and in particular, the rapidly increasing rate of juvenile crime in the declining older areas.

At the same time as the Urban Aid Programme was being prepared in the Community Relations Department of the

Women and children first

The idea was an old one and was firmly based on capital's continuing need for a healthy, well ordered workforce. The Beveridge Report of 1942 had made it clear:

In the next thirty years housewives and mothers have vital work to do in ensuring the adequate continuance of the British race and of British ideals in the world.
The Beveridge Report

Clearly by the 1960s the state judged women to be failing in their onerous, unpaid task and decided to take action. The Ingleby Report was followed between 1960-65 by the Morrison Committee on the Probation Service, the Royal Commission on the Police, reports by the Home Office Advisory Council on the Treatment of Offenders, the Longford Committee Report, *Crime; A Challenge to us all,* which recommended the setting up of Family Service Units, and the Royal Commission on the Penal System, all of which dealt with aspects of juvenile as well as adult crime. The Home Office report on *The Child, the Family and the Young Offenders* (1965) took up some of the points relating to the family made by the Ingleby Report:

The causes of delinquency are complex, and too little is known about them with certainty. It is at least clear that much delinquency – and indeed many other social problems – can be traced back to inadequacy or breakdown in the family. *The right place to begin, therefore, is with the family.* (our emphasis)
The Ingleby Report

The Seebohm Report on Local Authority and Allied Personal Services, which had been given the brief 'to review . . . what changes are desirable to secure an effective family service', was published in 1968 and recommended the reorganisation of social service departments in order to provide more integrated and co-ordinated services, as well as an increase in Community Development programmes.

Community control

It is clear then that, within Home Office thinking, the family and crime were inextricably linked. The rising rate of delinquency was an indication that the family was failing in its task of rearing law abiding citizens. In addition to improving the methods of dealing with offenders themselves through the police and the courts, new ways had to be found to tackle the problem at source. The Community Development Project was to put this thinking into action. Established as an experiment in new ways of helping the family it was to use the 'community' as a focus for mobilising informal social control mechanisms, rather than the individual or the family in isolation. The police were involved in the planning stages of the Project and were prepared to work closely with it when established. Many CDPs were approached by the local constabulary with offers of assistance and co-operation in their early days. The North Shields CDP, for example, in addition to

receiving frequent informal visits from local police officers during its first year, also received specially compiled monthly lists of indictable and non-indictable offences reported in the project area. It was some time before the police realised the project was not using the information and stopped compiling and sending it.

The social control element behind the programme was in fact recognised and acknowledged from the start. At the 1969 Ditchley Park Conference, called to discuss CDP and the Inner Area Studies in the light of the American Poverty Programme's experience, there was the following exchange:

Miss Cooper (Chief Inspector, Children's Department, Home Office) said that in both the British and American plans there appeared to be an element of looking for a new method of social control – what one might call an anti-value, rather than a value. 'Gilding the ghetto' or buying time, was clearly a component in the planning of both CDP and Model Cities [the US Poverty Programme].

Miss Stevenson (Department of Social and Administrative Studies, Oxford University) went along with this, pointing out that disordered behaviour in communities represented a nuisance to authority as well as presenting an idealistic challenge to administrators. She suggested that social workers were also interested in control, as much as the administrators. But the essence of CDP, as an example of hopefully progressive treatment, was the belief that people would respond to care, if they were not too frightened to do so. In other words, *one of its aims was to prove that there was an alternative to imposed control as a solution to social problems.* [our emphasis]
Minutes of the Ditchley Park Conference, 1969

The Home Office played this prominent role in the Poverty Programme precisely because family and community had been identified as important starting points in the fight against crime. Small amounts of money spent on family and community support might prevent much larger sums being wasted later on extra police and new prisons. As Seebohm put it

It makes no sense to us, either on humanitarian grounds or in terms of sheer economics, to allow young children to be neglected physically, emotionally or intellectually. By doing so, we not only mortgage the happiness of thousands of children, and the children they will in turn have, *but also pile up future problems and expense for society into the bargain.* [our emphasis]
The Seebohm Report

The idea of 'seed money' which would then have a 'multiplier effect' has been the favourite notion of Urban Aid and throughout, it has been heavily involved in financing projects relating to juveniles. In the very first phase of the programme, children's homes were one of three specified projects which would be financed and in subsequent phases a wide variety of projects geared towards the actual or potential young offenders were supported. These ranged from adventure playgrounds and playschemes to, in later years, intermediate treatment projects and other alternatives to residential treatment for young offenders.

The theme of family and community support was closely intertwined with another: race, racial tension, and race relations were a constant refrain in the Home Office poverty projects, and for similar reasons. Racial tension can lead to violence and disorder while unemployed black teenagers might seek to take out their frustrations on white society in general.

Fear of violence

It was not just the plight of the immigrants themselves which was the cause of the state's concern, but the effect of their presence upon the already aggrieved white population as a potential spark for violence. Alex Lyon, speaking to Parliament as Minister for State at the Home Office about the deprivation initiatives, made the position clear:

The problem [of urban deprivation] is complicated by the fact that a great many of those who suffer in these areas of deprivation are black and immigrant *and, therefore, add to the deprivation felt by the indigenous population of these areas.* They add newness, inadequacy of language and the cultural differences which go to make up racial discrimination within our inner cities.
Hansard, 29.7.74 [our emphasis]

Successive governments throughout the 1960s had taken the point. No longer short of cheap labour as the industrial shake-out proceeded, the policy they adopted to deal with this threat was to cut down on coloured immigration. With it went limited anti-discrimination legislation and attempts to dispel and pre-empt radical political organisation amongst the black population already here by setting up the Community Relations Commission and its network of community relations councils. Several of the poverty initiatives, especially Urban Aid reflected a similar low-key policy of directing limited resources into a variety of programmes aimed at making immigrant integration easier through such projects as language centres, hostels for West Indians, and generally improving facilities for both black and white in these urban areas through the provision of playschemes, nursery facilities and similar schemes. While the main emphasis went on keeping more blacks out of the country the home situation was being kept in hand.

Only a stone's throw from Liverpool *(left)* to Londonderry *(right)*? For the state the use of the army was a last resort *(far right).*

Urban warfare

... If there were to be in one of our big cities a situation such as that which obtained in Watts in Los Angeles at one time in recent American history, and if a similar pattern were to spread throughout our major cities, we would not have a President's commission to consider it; we would have Select Committees and questions in the House, and we would probably debate the subject ad nauseam.
Hansard, Alex Lyon 29.7.74

Alex Lyon and others too may have used the image of American race riots to emphasise the need for improvement of conditions in the cities, but there were examples much nearer home of what could happen in declining areas when a particular section of the population is consistently exploited and discriminated against. Northern Ireland, simmering in the late sixties had finally exploded into uncontrolled violence. Clearly a situation of far greater mass and organised 'civil disorder' than anything occurring in Britain in recent history, it couldn't be forgotten that the latest 'troubles' were sparked off by Catholic civil rights demonstrations about discrimination in housing allocation and similar issues.

At first attempts were made in Northern Ireland to use both the Community Relations programme and Urban Aid to dispel the mounting tension between Catholics and Protestants in the early 1970s. The Northern Ireland Community Relations Commission, established in 1970, developed a programme of community development which in some areas managed to get Catholics and Protestants to work together over common issues like bad housing. But the Stormont Government had no interest in encouraging such work and within two-and-a-half years both the chairman and the director of the Commission had resigned and the Commission was closed down in 1974.

With its low-profile approach discredited, the state was obliged to rely even more on the army to quell disorder, restore control and maintain some sort of calm in which the economic status quo could be shored up and a political solution explored. **But despite six years of immense cost and effort the army has been no more successful than the soft arm of the state in 'solving' the Northern Ireland 'problem'. Today the situation there is worse than in 1970. The obvious lesson is that quite apart from making the state's interests less conspicuous and costing far less, prevention is better than repression because it is more** *successful.*

Above: dismantling barricades. In action in Northern Ireland the army proved expensive, unpopular and not notably successful. Any long term national strategy called for more effective 'soft' police *(below)*

Soft option

It is clear that the Home Office involvement in the Urban Deprivation Programme reflects much more than concern for the welfare of the poor in this country. For the state, urban poverty means crime, juvenile delinquency, and in cities with large immigrant communities, potential race riots. The Home Office programmes represented to a large extent an attempt to breathe new life into the crumbling institutions of the family and the community in order to mobilise cheap, informal social control mechanisms. If the development of 'community identity', 'self-respect', 'parental authority' and 'self-help', could not stem the tide of vandalism and racism, the traditional law enforcement agencies, the police and the courts, would have to solve the problem. But it would be at much greater cost and would also represent a set-back for the governing idea that Britain can remain an orderly, self-disciplined society, free of violence, discrimination and crime without fundamental changes to the existing economic structure. Above all there was no guarantee, as the Northern Ireland situation had shown, that these more overt methods of control would be successful.

Army in Ulster 'needs plimsolls rather than boots'

By Chris Ryder

THE POLICE are a step nearer taking control of peace-keeping operations in Northern Ireland following a week of growing criticisms of the army's heavy-handed tactics

Senior police and army officers are already locked in discussions with government security advisers over ways of making the army subordinate to the Royal Ulster Constabulary, now believed essential to future peace in the province.

on an orders system, with officers handing instructions down the line. In contrast, the constable is taught to use his own initiative.

The unit blamed for much trouble by RUC officers is the Royal Military Police, described sometimes as the Royal Meddling Police.

As part of the Government's policy to Ulsterise security, troops were redeployed in many areas last spring and the RMP took over support duties for the

7 Ruling ideas

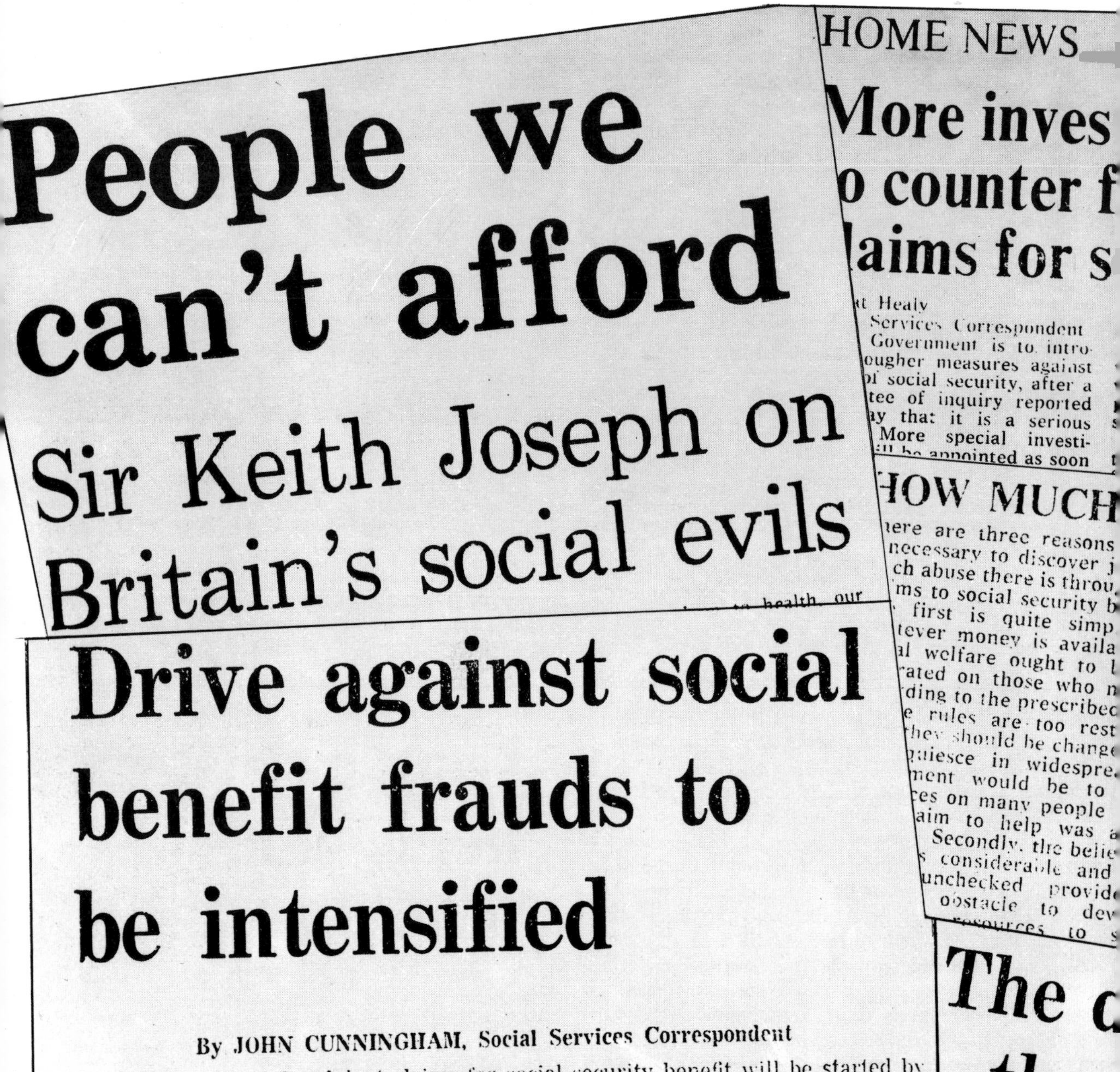

People we can't afford

Sir Keith Joseph on Britain's social evils

Drive against social benefit frauds to be intensified

By JOHN CUNNINGHAM, Social Services Correspondent

A drive against fraudulent claims for social security benefit will be started by the Government after the Fisher Committee's inquiry on abuse. But Sir Keith Joseph yesterday rejected the commitee's proposal to curb the methods used to spy on unsupported women suspected of drawing benefit illegally because they are living with a man.

No survey of the extent of abuse was made because the committee's brief was to

More inves
o counter f
laims for s

t Healv
Services Correspondent
Government is to intro-
ougher measures against
of social security, after a
tee of inquiry reported
ay that it is a serious
More special investi-
ill be appointed as soon

HOW MUCH

here are three reasons
necessary to discover j
ch abuse there is throu,
ms to social security b
first is quite simp
tever money is availa
al welfare ought to l
ated on those who n
ding to the prescribec
e rules are too rest
hey should be change
uiesce in widespre,
ment would be to
es on many people
aim to help was a
Secondly, the belie
s considerable and
unchecked provide
obstacle to dev
esources to s

The o
the

y housing estates n
ies and new h

50

Robert Carr made it clear that the urban problem was more than just crime at the tip of the iceberg; there was *social ferment lying beneath*. In revitalising informal community and family methods of social control to fight crime the Home Office would of course be dealing with that social ferment as well, but not necessarily. Crime is an essentially disorganised method of hitting back at a social structure. It is troublesome, destructive and expensive to the state, but it is not revolutionary. For the state, the greater danger by far is the possibility of systematically *organised* political revolt. In Northern Ireland the civil disorder which the British Army had been brought in to control was a reflection of organised political opposition to the Ulster State. It could happen in this country too.

Carr's theme was the old, old fear — one of the driving forces behind the welfare state and the source of many concessions to the working-class. It had been expressed many times before, among others by Sir John Gorst, a Tory MP of the 1880s and an advocate of the Settlement Movement, a nineteenth century precursor of CDP

 Modern Civilisation has crowded the destitute classes together in the cities making their existence thereby more conspicuous and more dangerous. These already form a substantial part of the population, and possess even now, though they are still ignorant of their full power, great political importance ... Almost every winter in London there is a panic lest the condition of the poor should become intolerable. The richer classes awake for a moment from their apathy, and salve their consciences by a subscription of money ... The annual alarm may some day prove a reality, and the destitute classes may swell to such a proportion as to render continuance of our existent social order impossible.

His contemporary, Charles Booth, made a subtler point

 ... The impression of horror that the condition of this class makes upon the public mind today is out of all proportion to that made when its actual condition was far worse, and consequently the need to deal with the evils involved becomes more pressing.
Life of the people in London, Vol 2, Charles Booth, 1891.

One of the problems for the state in the context of the 1960s, as opposed to the 1880s, was just this: that the new manifestations of urban poverty would focus attention upon the continuing class nature of a society that was supposed to have left such problems far behind. The community approach might be useful in reducing crime, but because it would also bring people together to discuss problems, it might also result in them taking collective action — possibly radical action. Indeed, the experience of CDP workers in areas of industrial decline very quickly led them to raise fundamental issues about the distribution of wealth and resources within society and encourage the tenants with whom they worked to do the same.

To some extent it was recognised that this polarisation into THEM and US with all its political implications had already taken place and was continuing to perpetuate itself. A Home Office paper commented

People living in deprived areas are often much more successful in communicating grievances amongst themselves, building them up into *symbols of their own social isolation,* than in communicating with the services who could help them.
CDP Objectives and Strategy, 1970

ors soon in drive
ulent
l security benefit

ny, was partial. The took evidence from departments, including MPs, and ral offices of the De- of health and social employment.
the report criticized ment of Health and

mendation to give priority to cases where non-disclosure of regular and substantial earnings are suspected, and will be making some changes in the "four-week rule" applied to some unemployed men and in cohabitation cases.
The committee had no doubt that non-disclosure of earnings the most offensive and

OCIAL WELFARE ABUSE

though not all of which the Government have accepted, but conclude that "in general the Departments have adopted sensible measures and have made good and economical use of the resources available to them for the prevention and detection of abuse". But they do not say just how much abuse there is. They are clearly concerned at its extent and say that "substantial sums of money are misappropriated each year". But they do not estimate how much or suggest how high a proportion of applicants may be involved. They conducted no surveys themselves did not ask the Government

dations which have rejected, believe that it to have a survey without invading innocent people. the moment are fined to those peo some degree of arisen.

There is force i It is right for any official agency to careful of p a plethora of sur confidential inves would be require tainly not be accep the ordinary proc

ived children ir
nd new slums

The problem was, as Derek Morrell, architect of CDP, put it at the meeting to discuss setting up the Coventry Project, how 'to help the people of Hillfields to frame realistic aspirations and enable them to attain the means to realise them'.

But what were those 'realistic aspirations' and how were the people of Hillfields — and others living in similarly run-down industrial areas — to be encouraged to direct their energies towards these rather than other, possibly more radical objectives?

Open repression through police and army could be used as a last resort in times of crisis, but for a supposedly democratic state the issue was not simply one of maintaining control by whatever means possible. Equally important was the need to maintain *consent,* to win public agreement to the official version of events. Not only was there the huge task of convincing all those outside the affected areas that all was well or going to be well, but the working-class people within those areas had also to be convinced, against all their own experience, that their poverty was the consequence, not of their class situation in relation to the development and needs of capital, but of other factors which appear to have no connection with that relationship. The definition of what the problem really was, and thus how it could be solved — through the framing of 'realistic aspirations' — was a task of major importance.

Back to school 1967 new Essex university and some new (police) students. More educated government was called for

Defining the problem

The 1960s saw the state turn to the thriving academic industry of the social sciences for a new framework to explain urban poverty. With education expanding and the social sciences going from strength to strength there was no shortage of respected academics who could run the commissions of enquiry and produce the reports that would set the tone for state policy. Nor was there any shortage of social science graduates to staff the new poverty programmes. But their task was not an easy one. In 1969 at the personal request of Harold Wilson an Anglo American conference was called at Ditchley Park, to compare CDP and EPA with their enormous American counterpart the US Poverty Program. High on the agenda at the conference was the idea that social science had so far failed to deliver a reliable 'macro-theory' that could be used to provide the public with explanations about the urban problem and that this failure might be a basis for the public 'witholding consent'. The social scientists were unfavourably compared with the economists — this was 1969 remember —

. . . the success of the economist in being absorbed into the political system lay not in his capacity to predict effects, but in his capacity to generate a consensus about which results were worth achieving.
Minutes of the Ditchley Park Conference, J. Rothenburgh

The economist had been able to build up a framework of theory that commanded widespread support and acceptance irrespective of its accuracy. The restructuring of British capitalism to ensure profitability was meeting with little opposition, although it was quite clearly not in the interests of people in the older industrial areas who saw their jobs being lost and their neighbourhoods declining. Why shouldn' the social scientists do the same and provide the state and particularly local government — which was having to pick up the pieces on the ground — with a rational objective and scientific research framework in which to develop solutions to the urban problem?

So the poverty initiatives emphasised survey techniques, statistical analysis and computer models. With touching faith the social scientist, with his finely calibrated measuring instruments, was expected to provide the precise answers to the problem.

[Evaluation] will continue throughout all subsequent phases, the object being to describe as accurately as possible what was done, when and by whom, with what expected results, and with what actual results, and hence when and how maximum return can be obtained for a given effort!
CDP: Objectives and Strategy September 1970

The theories current at the time centred on the notion of the 'culture of poverty', the idea that people inherited poverty, not because they were victim of the process of industrial decline but because there was something about them, their lifestyle, their values, that made them unable to take advantage of the opportunities available to them. It was this idea that the social scientists were to pass on through the poverty programme. Nor was it any new departure for the state. The Charles Booths and other social reformers of the nineteenth century, though self-motivated rather than state-paid enquirers, had served exactly the same purpose for the state then in furnishing explanations of what was happening to people in general and the working class in particular. What was different about this period was that because of the development of social science as a pseudo-scientific discipline in the post war period the sophistication and complexity of the explanations available had taken on a new lease of life.

Social scientists no longer needed to speak of the 'wretched, defrauded, oppressed, crushed human nature lying in bleeding fragments all over the face of society . . . ' (Colman, 1845) nor did the media have to operate with the crude explanations used by the Church in the nineteenth century

The rich man in his castle,
The poor man at his gate,
God made them high and lowly
and ordered their estate.
All Things Bright and Beautiful.

Instead they had the 'objective' scientific language of multiple deprivation and stratification systems to draw on and had developed complicated methods of proving that the class division between labour and capital no longer exists.

It was this ideology or system of ideas which the state mobilised in the form of the Poverty Programme to counter the day to day experience of working class people in the inner cities. The initiation of the different poverty initiatives was itself part of the process. The existence of special projects, government departments etc. to deal with the 'cycle of deprivation', 'social pathology' and their like clearly proved that these things must exist. The institutions were the definition made concrete.

'A minority'

CDP is based on the recognition that although the Social Services cater reasonably well for the majority, they are less effective for a minority who are caught up in a chain reaction of related social problems.
Home Office Press Release, 16.7.69.

Thus, the CDP brief carried home the idea that there's nothing wrong with the social services, but there is a minority who fall outside its efficiency. Built into the National Project's very existence, it's twelve small area teams, was the proof that the unlucky minority live in isolated pockets dotted around the country in what are in effect very special circumstances. These were the 'areas of special social need' constantly referred to by the Home Office and the Department of the Environment. This idea of poverty affecting only small groups in marginal areas is a powerful one for it immediately reduces the scale of the problem. It also carries the implication that those who live outside these areas share no common interests or problems with the

deprived within. The working class are effectively split into two and the scene is set for convincing those within that their problems have nothing to do with wider economic and political processes.

Drawing fixed boundaries around an area demonstrates the smallness of the problem. This is particularly misleading in inner city areas, but it is a good example of how the problem can be defined concretely for the local population. The boundary immediately sets them aside from the rest of the inner city, as small yet special. It turns them inwards and discourages them from seeking unity with neighbouring communities with identical problems.

Although the government has always stated that its projects were experimental, the small area focus has certainly diverted attention away from the scale of the issues.

The CDP Areas: tiny areas deflecting attention from a national map of inequality

Liverpool Inner Area Study estimate that the inner cities of the large conurbations alone house 3,800,000 deprived people, or 7% of the entire population. Plowden wanted to see 10% of the country's children in EPAs by 1971 — an estimate that has been made redundant by Department of Education's insistence that it was for local education authorities to decide their own EPA boundaries. Yet when Birmingham, for example, wanted to designate 191 schools for 'educational priority' it was forced to cut this total drastically as it represented almost half the total number *allowed* for the whole country!

Once poverty and exploitation have been defined as marginal it follows logically that only minor adjustments are needed to make it go away. The assumption that the policies of government and the exercise of economic power are determined by the interplay of separate interest groups in society is supported without question. If marginal groups are excluded through imbalances in the democratic and bureaucratic system this just has to be remedied by the proper representation of all groups in the political process. So we get 'positive discrimination'. A central notion in both EPA and CDP, the basic idea is familiar: by making special efforts in particular areas or with particular groups of people a basis for 'equal opportunity' will be laid, and the normal paths open for achievement will be established. But this idea was very quickly challenged. 'Positive discrimination' touched the state's Achilles heel in implying provision of greater resources, a concession it was unable to make in the late sixties because of the economic situation. So the later Poverty Programme changed its tune and sang of the need to 'prioritise needs' instead.

Technical solutions

But whatever the particular conception of the problem, the state's failure to deal with poverty is always presented as primarily a technical or administrative one. There is a continuing emphasis on management techniques — 'area management', 'community development', 'co-ordinated social plan' and most recently 'an urban deprivation plan' The implication is that the problems can be dealt with easily enough, once the right method or combination of methods have been found. Real solutions are seen to lie, not in the realm of politics, nor in the provision of extra resources, but in improving administrative practice with modern techniques, like programme budgeting, corporate management, computers and cost benefit analysis. In this scenario there is no room for questions of conflicts, or debate about the fundamental issues involved. The ineffectual policies of the state are obscured by the apparent rationality of the way problems are to be dealt with.

In Comprehensive Community Programme schemes for instance, CCP staff will draw up a plan for the area, prioritising needs and suggesting ways in which resources can be re-allocated within the local authority. The basic political question of much-needed *extra* resources is

excluded by this approach. Even within the illusion of political response created by methods such as area management and CCPs, technical solutions involving no basic structural changes, are simply providing a diversion from the real issues.

Social pathology

Although the major cause of poverty during the sixties was the decline of the industrial base of the older areas, few of the early poverty initiatives mention this fact. Instead poverty was called 'deprivation'. It was a problem of people, not of industrial change, and in case anyone was still in doubt a typical example would be thrown in.

. . . ill-health – financial difficulties – children suffering from deprivation – consequent delinquency – inability of the children to adjust to adult life – unstable marriages – emotional problems – ill-health and the cycle begins again.
Home Office Press Release, 16.7.69

In sociology literature this kind of description is known as a 'social pathology' model and at times the whole purpose of the poverty projects takes on a clinical connotation. The metaphor of the scientific experiment is implied in instructions about how to set up action projects:

There are extremely intricate problems of measuring cause and effect in social action programmes, and the planning of project activities in each area will, therefore, need to be under-pinned by a research design which makes the social action amenable to evaluation by research methods.
CDP Objectives and Strategy September 1970

and eventually it surfaces in the Neighbourhood Schemes where one of the aims is to 'act as a laboratory for CDP ideas as they develop'.

In the laboratory scientific rules must be obeyed. Dependence on the social services, for example, is viewed as some independent variable quite separate from any other factors affecting the people. The welfare state could solve people's individual problems, but when a significant number of those same people were concentrated in geographical areas — the old, the unskilled, the disabled, the unemployed left behind by the tide of industrial change — they become 'multiply deprived'. Whole families became caught in a 'cycle of deprivation' that was not only 'transmitted from generation to generation' like some hereditary disease but was also immune to the widely canvassed cure of 'equal opportunity'. Whole areas became affected, suffering from the 'social malaise' of 'urban deprivation'. The Lambeth Inner Area Study for instance talks of 'the environmental problems that arise in areas of poor and deprived people' and, like Booth, suggests that the problems can only be ultimately solved by 'dispersing the concentrations'.

That such areas can be identified by physical overcrowding, high unemployment rates, dereliction and decay is not disputed, the distortion comes as the focus is turned on the people not the environment or the wider structural causes. The implicit metaphor of illness is ever-present: people are 'suffering' from 'chronic' deprivation.

The continuing task

If this description seems to be a caricature, it is worth looking again at the criteria by which CDP research teams were meant to assess the effectiveness of their projects. These were indicators of improved family functioning, community functioning, personal care, childrearing practices, education and support for young children and physical conditions. Nowhere is there any mention of increased incomes or resources. The kind of change envisaged is mainly in anti-social *attitudes*: for example, reduced damage to houses, increased marriage and cohabitation stability, reduced delinquency and crime rates, reductions in dissatisfaction with employment and reduction in abuse of social services through fraud and voluntary unemployment.

While it is true to say that over the last two or three years, academics and others have mounted some challenge to these explanations of poverty and pointed to the wider social processes which determine low wages, bad housing and unemployment, the pathological metaphors have become increasingly popular in local government circles. One interesting example is a recent document produced by Newcastle Council entitled *Top Priority – Newcastle's approach to Poverty Areas*. Designed to put limited resources into twelve of the city's 26 wards (most of which had suffered cuts in the expenditure review of September 1975) the programme is described as an attack on 'stress'. Whilst admitting that the project would not eliminate the root causes of 'stress', the leader of the Council described it as a 'declaration of Newcastle's war on poverty', and many other cities have already made direct approaches asking for ideas and advice on similar approaches. The Department of Environment too has agreed to sponsor research into its value and to contribute £10,000 annually.

The task of ensuring that definitions of the problem are generally accepted and internalised by those who come into contact with the urban poor as well as the poor themselves is not an easy one. It is clear that the social pathology model is far from being universally agreed as a recent report from the Home Office's Urban Deprivation Unit and the Institute of Local Government Studies (INLOGOV), points out. Based on interviews with local authority officers in Birmingham and Nottingham it makes these wistful remarks:

our study has shown, not surprisingly, that there is no generally accepted definition of urban deprivation amongst those concerned with administering the local urban system. Many officers had not really considered the question previously . . . Most had some intuitive notion about 'urban deprivation' although they may have been uncertain about its validity . . .

Gilding the ghetto

These attempts to draw run-down working-class communities into a debate with local councillors and officials about their needs illustrates one of the starkest contradictions of the state's position. Here are areas where there has been a steady rundown of the traditional manufacturing industries – a process that has been deliberately encouraged by state policies. Although some new capital investment has been attracted for activities like warehousing and distribution, the general economic base and the supporting social infrastructure of the areas remains depleted. Yet, if left to rot even further, they begin to pose a direct political threat – both by their very existence and by their potential for social ferment.

So area management on the one hand and devices like information centres and community councils on the other, have been wheeled in to provide the illusion of political response. To quote Miss Cooper of the Home Office they were 'gilding the ghetto or buying time'.

In the past the tendency has been to see urban deprivation in physical terms. It is not surprising, therefore, that the policies developed to tackle the problems have been basically physical policies. The emphasis given to housing characteristics in particular leads to the emphasis on housing programmes as the means to combat urban deprivation. This physical bias is still strong. *Our analysis raises the important issue of whether more weight should be given to other factors, for example, family problems, lack of community spirit, lack of access and lack of power.* This would require major changes in the perspectives of many local authority and other agency officers. [our emphasis] *Local Government: approaches to Urban Deprivation*

Still, in 1976, the Home Office and the Department of the Environment-supported INLOGOV are concerned that too few local government officials see deprivation as a product of family and community deficiency.

The usefulness to the state of defining the urban problem to the residents of the older industrial areas as a sickness to be 'treated' hardly needs stressing. It fits neatly alongside the idea that it is a marginal problem to be solved by increased discussion – with the Neighbourhood Council acting as a surgery and the Area Management Team as medical consultants. The emphasis on 'tackling social needs' in isolation inevitably distracts attention from the root causes of the problem, by focusing attention upon personal deficiencies. The people themselves are to blame for the problems caused by capital. It was doubtless disagreement around this point which caused the instant resignation of the first director of the Glyncorrwg CDP – a child psychologist. Glwncorrwg is a small South Wales mining town with remarkable community spirit but unemployment of about 30% caused by the closure of all the pits in the valley. The Town Clerk and the psychologist had clearly different opinions about the nature of the problems in the area. After a stormy discussion, the psychologist caught the first train home and was never seen in the area again! Elsewhere, however, in inner Liverpool or Birmingham for example, the absurdity of the pathology model does not show up so clearly, although it has been implicitly or explicitly rejected by the staffs of all the EPAs, CDPs and Inner Area Studies.

Winning consent

At the Ditchley Park Conference Derek Morell, the civil servant who devised CDP gave this clear statement about the problem to which CDP and other poverty initiatives were to provide a solution.

The Chairman (Mr Derek Morrell) said the general context [of the discussion] was in his view the liberal-democratic process. It would be possible to discuss programmes and policy on the assumption that we had lost faith in this process, but he himself believed it had a highly creative future potential.

Looking, then, at the assumption about the role of government, or political process, it appeared to him that there were two principle ones to be considered. First, that the prime object of government was to maximise the total supply of welfare (in its British sense, not American) and, second, to produce a more equitable distribution of welfare. Inevitably, there was conflict between these two aims . . . Some might take the view that only a socialist solution could reconcile the two, but this basis was not open to the conference, whose task was to consider how progress could best be made, piecemeal, along both paths simultaneously. Legitimacy for a policy of reconciliation could be sought in the process of obtaining consent, and the painstaking accumulation of evidence . . . the role of the social scientist was to produce evidence, while the role of the politician or administrator was to generate consent . . . There was no doubt that this was very difficult. The whole process was wide open to manipulation, and involved practical problems of the transfer of power, from the 'haves' to the 'have-nots' – power, in the sense of the ability to effect or resist change. Even success, in this process, might be dangerous, and could destroy consent. But today's problem was not success, rather that consent might be withheld, because of accumulating evidence of failure.
Ditchley Park conference, 1969

Providing the definition of the problem alone was not enough. If people were to believe in these explanations there had also to be a solution. Here the answer was ready to hand: social democracy could be made to work. In fact it was of vital importance to the state that social democracy should be seen as able to provide a solution because in these areas of urban and industrial decline people already appeared to have lost faith in it. The turnout of electors at the local Council elections, low in the best of areas, was typically very low indeed in these areas. Yet as the Redcliffe-Maud Report warned

If local self-government withers, the roots of democracy grow dry. If it is genuinely alive, it nourishes the reality of democratic freedom.

Participation and making local councillors more efficient were the ways in which belief in the political system — and thus the economic structure underlying it – could be restored. The need for *responsive* local government and for people to *participate* more was a constant theme of many of the official reports of the sixties, picking up and turning to their advantage the contemporary demand coming from students and the trade union movement for more

participation in education and in industry, in the sense of more control. Public participation was embodied in the planning legislation of 1968 and the 1968 Housing Act which gave local authorities the power to declare General Improvement Areas. It was also a theme running through the early Poverty Programme — the Urban Aid and the Community Development Projects were explicitly aimed at developing self help and a new generation of local leadership which could then be involved in participating in local government decision-making.

The role of councillors was also a subject for discussion and experimentation in reports and programmes. The Bains Report (1972) suggested that councillors should become more involved with policy and less with the parish-pump. The brief of the Area Management Trials of 1974 included the provision of a framework in which elected members can relate council policies to local case-work and vice-versa. They were also to explore whether 'elected members find their role in area management a satisfying one providing a perspective against which they can better judge the local impact of council policies in each subject area'. (*DoE Press Release,* 6.9.74)

In 1974 in another circular (LG4/743/43) the Department of the Environment encouraged the setting up of Neighbourhood Councils. Their functions were to include familiar ideas: they were to stimulate self-help, foster a sense of community responsibility and, most important, 'to represent to operational organisations (central and local government, firms with factories in the area, etc) the needs and wishes of the local community'.

The Department of the Environment's own poverty initiatives, however, showed a lot more interest in the new

ALL HANDS UP FOR NEIGHBOURHOOD

Winning consent: The old way *(left)* **Keith Joseph as Minister of Housing and Local government tours the 'slums' of Hackney, 1962. And the new:** *(right)* **neighbourhood council 'participation'**

Idea of area management. Liverpool's Inner Area Study described this as 'an attempt to bring parts of the City's administration closer to the people it is designed to serve, through the actions of elected members and officials working within a formal area management structure'. Local government would be brought to the people. Having got it there the people would be expected to join in its deliberations through Neighbourhood Councils and Community Forums. The Area Management Trials (1974) are expected to answer such questions as 'Does it help the council to relate more immediately and sensitively to the views of neighbourhood councils and other groups, and to help them to participate effectively, for example, in the planning process?'

Behind that illusion though the projects did have their uses – but for the state, not the people living in the older urban areas. For the state has a continuing need to keep its fingers on the working-class pulse to know what is going on particularly in those difficult unorganised sections of the working class where there are no established channels, unions, or leadership to deal through. It needed to know what to expect from the ghettoes and to have accurate information with which to update the diagnosis of the problems and so produce the next set of policies.

Despite the similarity of the different initiatives, the feedback process can be seen at work even within the space of the poverty programme of the last decade: the 'action research'

emphasis gives way to area management, 'positive discrimination' and to 'prioritising needs'. Even more clearly, the critical findings of CDP and some of the Inner Area Study reports with their insistence on the economic system as the root-cause of continuing poverty, can be seen today being fed back in mutilated form to the media via the 'structural' rhetoric of Peter Shore for example.

> The causes [of inner area decline] lie primarily in their relative economic decline, in a major migration of people, often the most skilled, and in a massive reduction in the number of jobs which are left . . . Many facilities in our inner urban areas need qualitative improvement, and some need total and often expensive replacement.
> Peter Shore, 17.9.76

while the old, now unpopular 'personal pathology' approach is faded into the background.

Keeping the initiative is essential to the state's success. It has to update its ideas and change definitions to keep abreast with critical comment, working-class pressure and the inevitable failure of its piecemeal measures, if it is to maintain its own credibility and public consent.

The wide range of opinions and ideas represented by the professionals working for the state (never wider perhaps than at the height of the poverty programme) all go to help this process of ideological renewal on its way. While they seek new state 'solutions' to the 'problems' in good faith and genuine concern the state has within itself a valuable reserve of alternatives to turn to. To the outside world they create the illusion that government is really trying to do something to alleviate the problems and that given the *right* ideas social democracy does work. As the needs of the poorer sections of the working class are defined as 'realistic aspirations' and the blame is diverted away from the real source and onto those who suffer the consequences of decline, the institutions of the state reorganise and revitalise themselves.

8 Managing

With money for the social services short, voluntary labour became
a key theme of 'community development'. The state had its eye
particularly on extending the unpaid work of women. *Below:* a
local mother 'helping' at Craiglielea Primary School nursery unit
in the Paisley CDP area. *Insert:* another idea from Sir Keith Joseph.

Sir Keith suggests 'substitute grannies'

Nowadays we hear a great deal about the need to save money and cut back public expenditure on the unproductive services'. In many ways this seems a far cry from the atmosphere of the sixties when the growth of public spending was at its peak. Yet by the time CDP and the Urban Programme were being set up there was already a growing concern in some parts of government that public spending was getting out of hand. How to cope with the 'bottomless pit' was already a central theme of the early poverty initiatives. And it has become the key note of the recent schemes, with their concentration on saving money co-ordination of services, cost-effectiveness and prioritising needs.

Today with the economic crisis considerably worsened the approach is out in the open. 'Explanations' of the economy are served up in the newspapers, on radio and television almost every day now. We know there is a 'crisis', we must all 'tighten our belts', we know about 'lack of investment', 'low productivity', unemployment. We are convinced that the 'national interest' is indeed our interest, even if it means unemployment and declining living standards for us and increased profits for the national and international corporations.

We know there is no money, and that what there is or can be found by cutting public services must go to restore industrial profitability. So it comes as no surprise that no resources can be found to increase jobs or improve facilities. Nor does it seem wrong to hear other government statements that resources are limited and the experiments are actually aimed at better use of existing resources, including the 'untapped resources of the community' rather than tackling the issues for those who experience poverty.

The later poverty initiatives with their open emphasis on management and re-allocation of resources and conspicuous silence about the issues of urban exploitation are in tune with the times. In the sixties, though, the basic concern about finding ways of saving money was being introduced into a very different ideological climate.

The state's main concern was the enormous increase in local authority spending. Central government, hardpressed by huge borrowing to maintain public spending, became concerned about the increase and took steps to integrate and control it within the total pattern of state spending, recommending a vast range of new management and technical devices to improve the local authorities' budgeting. But at the same time public expectations were high and had been encouraged to rise by the optimistic rhetoric of the fifties and sixties. People were expecting more from the Welfare State, especially in high cost services like housing and education. White collar workers were becoming tougher about pay increases; militancy worked, as traditionally respectable groups like the hospital workers found. More women going out to work meant increased demands for nursery care; the unpaid work they had done before — looking after the elderly and their sick relatives, as well as their children — put additional demands on local government services.

The government's own advisors, often echoing the wisdom of liberal academics, were also recommending increased spending. The official reports described earlier were designed to update the services organised by the state to maintain a healthy labour force, which also had the necessary manual and intellectual skill. They called, in effect, for extra spending. Milner Holland wanted more local authority housing in London; Plowden, more and better primary schools; Robbins, big increases in higher education; Seebohm, extra resources for the personal social services. The list was endless.

Alongside these reports, the government sponsored others to look at ways of updating local authority techniques of handling their burgeoning budgets. Maud, Mallaby and Bains, but particularly the last, recommended improved techniques that were already in operation in some local authority areas. There was clearly a need to extend and expand these services.

The poverty initiatives were primarily experiments with and on the residents of the older industrial areas. But they were also experiments with and on the local authorities themselves. Above all they were experiments *on behalf of* the central and local state. In this respect they were most important in providing a laboratory for both civil servants and local government officials to test out current and developing ideas not only about how to cut up the cake and distribute it, but how to get the best value for money. As ever the issue was presented as a problem of administration. The government however was quite clear about the political nature of resource allocation issues.

Managing through community development. The plan for Liverpool CDP

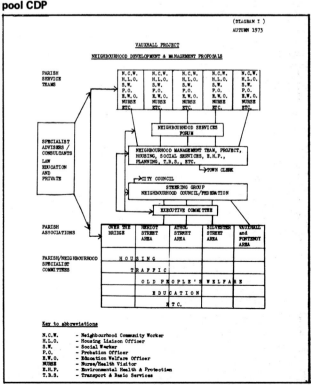

It would also be an essential part of the experiment to assess how far, and on what criteria of need, policies involving positive discrimination in the use of resources could be pursued without loss of financial control, and without provoking 'backlash' effects from other communities or areas of need. The latter consideration would be particularly important where the CDA [later CDP] contained a high proportion of immigrants: we should wish to include two or three such areas within the experiment.
Report of an Inter-Departmental Working Party, chaired by Derek Morrell, 21.5.68

Taken at face value it might seem that the state ignored the findings of its programmes, but with economic context and the real concerns of the state understood, it becomes clear that they were far from ignored. In fact the state has taken up the poverty programme suggestions in a systematic and highly selective way that reveals precisely its own interests. Recommendations to do with increased resource provision have been carefully ignored – the priority was not to improve the material conditions of the working class in the 'affected areas' in this way. But suggestions which have helped in the better management of urban problems without involving extra resources have been taken on board – the management of the poor is to be streamlined.

Co-ordination

The official wisdom of the sixties and to some extent today, is that there is a high risk of duplicating effort and cost in central and local state activity, unless there is strong co-ordination. Money might be wasted if, for example, social workers from two different sections went to the same family about different problems. The family and the local authority would benefit if all help and advice was organised through one social worker.

From this sort of simple and obvious example it was inferred that co-ordination was needed at all levels – between local authorities and voluntary agencies and groups, between local and central government and even between central government departments. Within the context of local government as a whole this idea was enshrined in 'corporate management'. The poverty initiatives focussed principally on the co-ordination of service delivery aspects of the local authority.

CDP, for example, following in the tradition of Seebohm, assumed that

. . . the quality of co-operation that is needed, especially in poor communities, requires the co-ordination of inter-service teams concerned with neighbourhood areas.
CDP: Objectives and Strategy September 1970

while the Department of the Environment considered that

In the past the attitude has been a series of fragmented decisions not properly co-ordinated and not bringing about the improvement of urban areas which is necessary.
Peter Walker, Secretary of State for the Environment, 1973

A 'total approach' was needed – an idea later redefined as area management – 'extending corporate management down to an area level'.

Briefly, in 1973, the Home Secretary, Robert Carr,

recognised that government urban deprivation policies themselves needed more 'comprehensive co-ordination'. This was what produced the Urban Deprivation Unit and in due course the CCPs too – the last word in co-ordination. Even Regional Planning Boards and central government departments were to be included.

Community productivity deal

But good co-ordination, at best, only provides an efficient baseline; and in most situations, as many local authorities have discovered, good co-ordination actually costs more. Much bigger savings can be effected by increasing productivity. In local government language this is called 'cost effectiveness'.

The focus of the poverty initiatives however was not on workstudy for social workers, teachers or planners, but on getting more out of the *community itself* and out of short, one-off, professionally-run schemes which would initiate voluntary work on a longer term basis. This 'multiplier effect' was the main principle behind Urban Aid and the EPA projects.

The theory is that an adventure playground, for example, employing one or two playleaders, will organise activities for the children which are useful because they keep the kids off the street. Meanwhile the parents of the children will get together initially as a playground committee but later to use it as a focus for other neighbourhood activities – Christmas parties, summer coach trips, visiting old people, fundraising for a community centre and so on. The Quality of Life Project was almost entirely about this kind of activity and there was an emphasis on *not* using local authority funds.

EPA, especially in Liverpool, was very involved in pre-school playgroups (which are usually run by local parents) and with the concept of the community school. This embraces Plowden's idea of teacher aides (teachers on the cheap) but also seeks to link up the community and the school curriculum. The spin-off for the state would be improved education standards – a continual concern as recent uproar about the 3Rs has shown. Indeed the overt philosophy of EPA was how 'to find the most economical way of getting the best results' *(Educational Priority Vol. 1* and the project concluded that 'pre-schooling is an outstandingly economical and effective device for raising education standards'.

CDP again echoes Seebohm with its aim of creating community spirit in order to

. . . take some of the load off the statutory services by generating a fund of voluntary social welfare activity and mutual help amongst the individuals, families and social groups in the neighbourhood, supported by the voluntary agencies.
CDP: Objectives and Strategy 1970

Urban Aid was to have a similar role

. . . the co-operation of parents in the running of the project can be of considerable importance in helping to foster the community spirit. The potential here is as yet largely untapped, and its value

should not be underestimated.
Urban Programme Circular No. 6 December 1971

Though none of the projects are explicit, it is clear that parents usually means mothers, and voluntary social welfare workers are always women. Although there were growing numbers of women going out to work there were still plenty at home who could be roped in as an alternative to employing full-time, paid nursery teachers or social workers.

The ideas of self help and participation, too, had a potential pay-off for local government. Re-creation of community identity and feeling could perhaps lead to informal pressures on tenants to maintain their houses in better condition. Community activity around children would perhaps encourage adults to keep a tighter rein on the young people and discourage them from vandalising public property. A conference called by the Northumbria Police in 1975 on vandalism specifically recommended that local councils should encourage the establishment of local community organisation for these reasons.

And although local government may not now be responding to central government initiatives on the Poverty Programme with as much enthusiasm as before, certain ideas have rubbed off and been incorporated into their structures. The number of community workers employed by the local state has increased considerably over the years since the beginning of the Poverty Programme. Their role, as with the Poverty Programme in general, has been and remains to help the local state to solve its problems of maintaining credibility in the eyes of the poorer section of the working class and to manage them and its services more efficiently.

Redirecting priorities

Whether these voluntary activities ever made or ever will make any substantial difference to state spending is impossible to assess. What is clear is that during the seventies local authority management has become the prime focus of the poverty iniatives. This goes hand in hand with increased government control of local authority spending. This year all expenditure has a fixed cash ceiling and local authority overspending is to be punished by deductions from next year's Rate Support Grants.

This trend has been accompanied by the new official recognition that only extra resources will solve the problems of the older industrial areas. As there are none, however, attempts are now being made to rob Peter to pay Paul — hoping of course that Peter will not notice until Paul can in turn be robbed. This is known as 'redirection of priorities' and has been the particular interest of projects concerned with area management and CCPs. The Home Office project is quite explicit:

In the present economic climate when new resources are unlikely to be available, such redirection will involve difficult decisions about priorities and it is these which the CCP is intended to inform. *Comprehensive Community Programmes: Home Office Note,* September 1975.

Self-management? committee members from the cellar youth project, Cleator Moor CDP

It is perhaps for this reason that local authorities seem reluctant to co-operate in setting up CCPs.

Area management, as discussed earlier, is concerned with participation and legitimating technical solutions for political problems. But the exercise is also about the 'allocation of resources' — both within the local authority and within the area. With the present cutback in public expenditure it seems likely that in almost every area the allocation will be downwards and that area management will be exploring instead what working-class communities are prepared to put up with — derelict schools OR unimproved housing OR minimal social services. Since it is not prepared to allow substantial expenditure on all three any more, it is important for the state to know which can be dropped with minimum opposition.

It would be a mistake, though, to think that the cuts in public spending represent a withdrawal on the part of the state after its heyday of expansion in the 1960s. It may represent a cutback in *spending,* there may be fewer and less adequate services for people who are poor, ill, in need of education or a home, but the tentacles of the state are not being retracted. This precisely is the usefulness of recent management developments.

Take for example the recent substantial cut in the Rate Support Grant for 1977-78. This withdrawal of funds does not mean that central government is reducing its involvement with, or control over, the local authorities, rather the opposite. It represents a strong central move to force all local authorities to restrict their spending in line with central policy. It is also an astute move, for any council wanting to maintain current levels of services will have to face its local constituency with an even greater rate rise than the 15% average now being predicted for 1977-8. With wages held down and prices rising it would be a brave local authority which would dare.

The decision, profoundly political, and devastating in its implications both for local authority workers and those most in need, is however presented as a technical one, an adjustment to the economic machine, a righting of balances. Within the local state, corporate management and similar techniques have done the same for countless other, smaller issues. Today's worsening situation finds large areas of decision-making transferred out of the realm of politics and into the hands of experts, reinforcing the notion of technical solutions and removing them from public debate. This in itself has been a major achievement in shoring up the power of the state, an achievement which has re-equipped the state to meet new pressures more efficiently.

Not only has the state reorganised as capital reorganised, but it has taken a lesson in management techniques from industry which makes it better prepared to meet the consequences of capital's activities.

Conclusion

The state's fight against urban deprivation has been exposed, like the 'emperor's new clothes', as empty rhetoric. But just as no one was foolhardy enough to laugh at the emperor, we too would be rash to disregard the reality behind the packaging of the Poverty Programme.

The basic dilemma for the state remains the same — how best to respond to the needs of capitalism on the one hand and maintain the consent of the working class on the other. Now in the mid-seventies the problems we have described over the last decade have become more acute. The economy is in crisis and desperate measures are being called for. The profitability of British industry can only be restored by a reduction in wages and living standards. As the state responds to the needs of capital, the scope of the problem experienced by the working class can no longer be explained as a marginal problem of the inner city and the blame put upon the inadequacies of the people living there. The working class as a whole is being affected by reductions in real wages, by the threat of unemployment and by the fall in the value of the social wage, as public sector cuts affect services of all kinds from transport to health to social services.

This is the wider reality which puts the Poverty Programme in its proper perspective. For what kind of a 'Welfare' State is it which, at a time when economic recession is causing additional hardship, particularly among the people living in 'areas of special social need', cuts back the services on which people depend. Planned in the first place in order partly to protect working class people from the harsher consequences of unfettered capitalism, its very structure is now being dismantled to help shore up an economic system that has patently failed to provide decent living standards for all. It

is not surprising, then, that in the final analysis the 'deprivation initiatives' were not about eradicating poverty at all, but about managing poor people.

Cracks in the state

The story of the Poverty Programme reveals the nature of the state's interests and activities quite clearly. The Programme has evolved as a testbed for new ideas and strategies for dealing with the working class. As such, it also provides a framework both for understanding better the variety of ways in which the state operates and for locating the weaknesses and contradictions within the state's structures and activities. In this report we have concentrated on drawing out the broader strands of the state's interests and objectives. In doing so we have run the risk of presenting the state as a monolithic force.

As workers for the state ourselves, we are aware of the extent to which this is an oversimplification. Our experience in CDP makes us acutely conscious of the range of opinions represented within the state structures. The state has now embraced the liberal conscience of the nineteenth century philanthropists as well as the social-democratic values of people like Beveridge. As a result we have found clear political differences, for instance, between council employees and councillors, between central and local government, civil servants and MPs, council committee chairmen and 'backbenchers' in their own parties. It is also clear, with increasing public expenditure cuts, that of the workers employed by it are in opposition. Many of these workers, those at the bottom end of the state hierarchy, are also the ones at the receiving end of the Welfare State — who live in the declining areas, who need the services most and find them least often provided. It has used them for years as cheap labour to perform manual jobs in the hospitals and local services. At the professional level, too, there is an increasing gap between the level of resources which teachers, nurses, social workers, public health inspectors and others need in order for them to do their job to their own and their clients' satisfaction and what the state is now prepared to fund. The resistance of state workers to low wages and, more recently, to the threat of redundancy and increased workloads yet lower standards, has been one of the most important recent developments in working class organisation.

But the struggle of state workers is not simply about wages and conditions of work, or restoring the level of services of a few years ago. The issues raised in this report show that it has to be about the content of the work we do, too. We have already shown how the state, in order to maintain control over a situation, defines the everyday problems experienced by people in terms which reflect *its* needs and interests. Thus the Poverty Programme, although arising from the problems of poverty and exploitation experienced by those living in the older declining areas, was not developed in order to solve or alleviate *their* problems, but to help the state meet its problems in dealing with these people. In the same way the successful working class demands for better living conditions, whether housing, health services or education, have in the past been translated into the language and needs of the state. They may be 'our' hospitals, schools and council houses, but they have been shaped by the state according to *its* interests, the interest of maintaining the necessary conditions for capital to flourish, not the interests of those who use the services. Questions about the kind of services and whom they are for, are central to furthering the interests of both the workers, who provide the services, and the consumers on the receiving end, for they are often the same people.

For CDP workers, the contradictions involved in being state employees paid to analyse the causes of poverty, meant that effective organisation of all the twelve projects, across the institutional barriers drawn up by the Home Office, was essential both to protect our jobs and to extend our understanding of the problems we were employed to deal with. This has enabled us to develop our analysis of the reality which faces people in the areas of industrial decline and reject the definitions of the problem handed to us by the state. We have only been able to do this because at the same time we fought for the right to control our work — what we do, for whom we are doing it and why. Breaking the geographical boundaries — through inter-project meetings and the CDP Workers' Organisation — not only helped us to reject the small area focus we had been given, but also to resist Home Office attempts at control, when our employers reacted to this analysis.

For other state workers, working in the health service, public transport, education, housing and other services, there are possibilities for similar activity once the contradictory nature of state services is recognised and the decision is made to work towards providing a service in the interests of the working class, not capitalism and the state. This means not just fighting against the diversion of resources away from the public services but also acting collectively to change the structures through which these services are provided so that both workers and consumers have a service which is geared towards their needs and over which they have control.

Acknowledgements

Birmingham Evening Mail, 3 (bottom left); *Birmingham Post,* 2 (bottom left), 6 (middle right) 9.11.76; Camera Press, 3 (top left), 8 (top right), 15 (top left), 44; *Coventry Evening Telegraph,* 4 (right) 15.2.69; Christopher Davies (Report), 35 (right), 41 (top right); *Evening Standard,* 26; *Guardian,* 4 (right) 11.7.69, 42 (bottom left) 25.11.66, 58, 28.6.73, 58, 22.7.75, 50, 3.5.72, 50, 29.3.73; Henry Grant, 11 (top right), 12 (bottom left), 22 (bottom right), 48; Kathy Henderson, 40 (top right); Keystone, 4 (bottom left), 9 (top left), 18, 30 (left), 35 (left), 37 (bottom right), 38, 49 (top left), 49 (top right), 52 (bottom left), 56 (top right); Labour Party Photograph Library, 8 (bottom right), 8 (bottom left), 34 (bottom right); *Labour Weekly,* 6 (top right), 23.1.76. 6 (middle right) 7.11.75; Manchester *Guardian,* 6 (bottom right) 22.1.76; Mary Elgin International Freelance Library, 47; Mary Evans Picture Library, 39; *Observer,* 50, 20.10.74; Popperfoto, 13 (bottom right); John Sturrock (Report), 31 (left); *Sunday Times,* 2, 28.11.76, 49 (bottom right) 17.10.76; *The Times,* 6 (bottom right) 22.1.76, 27, 30.1.67, 50, 29.3.73; Topix, 8 (top left), 14 (top right); *Voice of Stamshaw,* 57, 7.74; Andrew Wiard, (Report), 63 (top).

CDP Photographs

Nick Birch, 21, 32; Simon Danby, 61 (bottom); Robert Golden, 45 (bottom right); Nick Hedges, 5, 23, 33; Larry Herman, 19 (left), 30 (right), 58; Derek Massey, 20, 34, 35; Roger Perry, 36.

Published February 1977 by the CDP Inter-Project Editorial Team, Mary Ward House, 5 Tavistock Place, London WC1H 9 Telephone 01-387 5126.

This report does not necessarily reflect the views of the Home Office or any of the local authorities.